HYMNS
OF
HOME

A Collection of Essays

Bill Bunn

Published by Bitingduck Press
ISBN 978-1-938463-35-8
© 2013 Bill Bunn
For information contact
Bitingduck Press, LLC
Montreal • Altadena
notifications@bitingduckpress.com
http://www.bitingduckpress.com
Cover image by Linda Bunn

Publisher's Cataloging-in-Publication data
Bunn, William [1963--   ]

 Hymns of home: a collection of essays/by Bill Bunn—1st
edition
   p. cm.

Contents—Personal reflections on family, environment, living
green and related topics

ISBN: 978-1-938463-35-8
[1. Family—Family Relationships. 2. Environment—human
ecology. 3. Green Revolution. 4. Nature and Nurture—
Environment.] I. Title

LCCN 2013930805

This book is dedicated the music of my life: my wife and family who made me want to write, and Moira Dann who helped me play my first notes.

CONTENTS

I

THE BIG, SHORT PARTY

ACTUALLY WISHED HE HAD started to kick and scream; it makes it so much easier when they kick and scream.

But he's a dedicated little boy, so he tries to take well most of what we throw at him. I watched him trying to manage his emotions as he contemplated me leaving him alone there. His chin trembled, and he blinked hard as I sat him down to take off his backwards boots, ones that he had proudly put on himself a few moments earlier. I watched his shoulders sag as the moment approached.

His body went limp as I removed his hat and coat. As soon as he was ready, he gave me a big hug and kiss, then went to the window as I prepared to leave him there. I stepped outside, moved toward the car, and then turned to him, to that place in the window where his face usually was.

He smiled weakly as I gave him my grin-and-bear-it smile—it's really facial advice. Then he started blowing kisses, as the tears rolled down his cheeks. I couldn't handle the sight anymore, so I turned and ran back to my car, afraid that if I turned to look once more, I'd quit my job to stay home and play with him forever.

As I drove away, my eyes averting my siren son, I noticed an angular pain in my soul, one I'd not felt very often. After a short session of emotional arithmetic, I could only locate one other occasion I felt this particular kind of painful longing: my grandfather's death.

He passed away when I was a teenager, and I remember struggling to understand what death meant in my lived experience. I couldn't understand the afterlife. How can you understand forever?

I felt claustrophobic thinking about what it might be like to be sleeping inside a coffin under the ground. Instead, I learned to believe that death was simply absence: he was "gone." That parting of ways, and lingering absence conjured this odd, and particularly sharp, sort of pain. Because I've learned to understand death as an absence, what my son and I suffered as we waved goodbye, was nothing more than a small dying, a death, an on-the-spot, makeshift funeral.

You could accuse me of being overly dramatic. I've accused myself of the same thing. I've taken my feelings to task, insisting that I get over this inappropriate emotion immediately.

But I can't.

And, now, I don't believe I'm being overly dramatic. Death and goodbye are the same thing, existentially speaking: my son was absent from my day, just as my grandfather is. My emotions, no matter how much I tried to jimmy them into seeing things another way, will not budge. They have marked this kind of occasion for me as a death.

So, death I must live with as I work through my professional day.

But, then, when the locks on my briefcase snap closed, I hop in the car to return to that home where I left him earlier in the day. What a miracle moment it is: The dead are brought back to life. I witness the resurrection once we make eye contact. The morning's shroud buries itself in our reunion, and death's permanent marks are wiped away for a moment. These milliseconds of joy have become one of my favourite instants.

Our reuniting is one moment of pure life, for in that moment death is completely erased. My time with my son has not yet become tinged with the weight of future goodbyes, nor the sly death of taking one another for granted: it is my complete, momentary appreciation of my son, without the thought of what may lie ahead. A complete celebration of life. A huge party, lasting two heartbeats.

As I have come to understand goodbye and hello and their profound significance in my life, I don't let those moments go unlived. I've given up resenting them and have embraced these daily deaths and resurrections.

These are some of the mundane miracles that bring a tear to my eye every time they happen, and hold me close to the root of what living is all about.

Originally published as "You say hello and I say goodbye" in the Globe and Mail, Facts & Arguments, June 1, 2000.

2

THE CHILD BEYOND THE DICTIONARY

SHE FUMBLES FOR MY ear.

When she finds it, she sets her lips on the outside of my ear breathing heavily into it as she thinks of something to say.

"Ummm," she starts, still waiting for words to arrive. Her hot breath rolls into my ear, filling it with sticky sound.

"Christmas... um... birthday party... um... presents... ah... grandma... candy store, suckers... and slides, swimming pool, dessert."

It's my two-year-old daughter, Elise. I sit and listen because I love how her secret feels in my ear, as her little hands dance on the back of my neck.

And I realize that she's giving me a precious gift, a string of her most-prized words, beaded sound, threaded on breath for my ears only.

She's the same one who always asks for me to whisper things into her ears, especially goodnight. My whisper isn't nearly as sticky. It's drier, I think, and the words I use don't burn beats on the eardrum.

She pulls my ear to her mouth again, as she remembers a fragment of another secret she can tell. "Baby soup," she says. I know her words translate to "bathing suit" in a grown-up vocabulary.

Her mouth strings syllables together in a way that no dictionary could track. As she talks, her secrets plant meaning in me. They take me where a dictionary cannot go, to the uncommon sense of what childhood means: childhood sounds like one of Elise's secrets.

Childhood looks like Elise does, after she dresses herself. "I do it myself," she insists as she slams the door to her bedroom. Then after a five-minute storm of huffs and puffs in a fabric fight, she emerges with a turtle-neck shirt, with her lithe, writhing middle somehow squeezed into the neck hole, the bottom of the shirt was dangling open around her neckline like a bell. A pair of Teletubbies panties, on backwards with the gusset hugging her left hip. "I did it myself," she says proudly.

I wear clothes just as they were supposed to be worn. I find no new way to wear my underwear, nor do I wear my shirt upside down simply because it's possible.

Sometimes Elise sits on my knee and presses her forehead against mine for a quiet chat. In the growing warmth between our bodies, I catch hints of apple juice and chocolate cake. I spy the sheen of apple juice flecked with brown cake crumbs swabbed generously around her mouth, lolling down the cape of her chin.

Forehead to forehead we sit, and I imagine she who smells of apple juice and chocolate cake smells strains of my day—photocopier, cold coffee, book mould.

On her cheeks are tears, ones that have fallen because she

has. She pokes one of her small fingers into a tear and holds it out for my tongue.

"Salty," she says. She watches me taste it as if she might see what salty looks like. Then, content with what she sees, she kisses me, and I taste mostly apple juice with a hint of chocolate. Again, I learn. Childhood is the taste of Elise's tear and the smell of a kiss of apple juice and chocolate cake.

Childhood feels like Elise's fresh-bathed skin. I watch her wiggle out of the bath, sink deep into a towel, and come and sit on my knee. I dry her hair. She's so clean, her skin is so young, she feels almost sticky again—sticky clean.

Now, she's fascinated with her belly button. She squeezes it from both sides with her hands. "Closed" she says. She lets go. "Open."

She feels her own skin with some sense of wonder, as though it feels new to her too. "You do it, Dad," she says. I lift my shirt and squeeze my belly button, and she says "Closed." I let it go and she says "Open." She squints at my recessed "inny" and looks down at her own again. She runs her finger inside my belly button and wiggles it, feeling the wound that began my childhood so long ago. It's scaled, and filled with lint.

I touch her belly button and she jumps as if the connection is still live. I feel the jolt as I touch her too, and pull away. The lesson is complete. I know what childhood means. She's taken me beyond the dictionary again.

A dictionary is a book of seeds. It contains the dry husks of words that have not yet rooted in living, waiting to find their meaning. The dictionary tells me nothing about how a word lives or finds a home in worlds. But I learn.

The word "childhood" grows up in me suddenly. I feel the senses of the word branch and bud in my brain.

And I tremble.

The word now lives in me.

Originally published as "From baby soup to bathing suit" in the Globe and Mail, Facts & Arguments, April 11, 2001.

3

AND THEY CALL IT
BUNGALOW LOVE

PETITE 1950s CHARACTER HOUSE, 3 bedrooms, seeks unattached young family for lasting, meaningful relationship.

It's a modest bungalow: 1,036 square feet, built in the winter of '55, in Calgary. Not much to look at. It has three bedrooms, a tiny bathroom, a small kitchen and a dining area cum living room, all of them small.

My main complaint with this bungalow is a lack of storage space. I once believed the builder was wooden-headed about storage. Now, I understand this bungalow furnishes us with the values and worldview of its time: it's a philosophy—assumptions of cement, arguments shaped in wood and plaster. For instance, the closet space is small because the 1950s builder was a material minimalist. Four or five suits, twice as many shirts, a pair of shorts and a housecoat were all a reasonably attired middle-class male needed, so closets, I think, seemed roomy at the time.

The storage accessory for the bathroom is a small three-shelved medicine cabinet. Room for a bottle of Aspirin, after-shave, Brylcreem, and a brush for me. Linda would share the Aspirin bottle, add some hairspray, perfume, and her own brush to the cabinet. With the room left over we could store Mercurochrome, gripe water and Band-Aids for the kids. These days, my doctor can overwhelm those three shelves by herself if she is in a prescriptive mood. And where do I put my collection of hair gel and vitamins?

Kitchen. The cupboards would comfortably house one collection of dishes, a set of pots and pans, spices, and a hand-held mixer. We own a bread machine, microwave, crock pot, meat slicer, food processor, waffle iron, coffee grinder (one hand-crank, one electric), French press, percolator, drip machine, cappuccino machine, kettle, two teapots, industrial mixer, deep fryer, electric fry pan, chicken cooker, turkey racks, the good dishes, pots and pans (a set and a half), and the everyday dishes.

After we first purchased the house, we tried to bring in a new, large, plushy four-cushioned couch. The way the front and back doors are designed, it wouldn't fit: end up, end down, upside down, angled, wedged sideways. Even with a professional mover on the job, it wouldn't go. So the couch went back to where it had come from.

This 1950s bungalow stands for its time, without excuse, embarrassment or compromise, although it's a bit curmudgeonly on its point. The house doesn't want us collecting things: it resists gadgets, whizmos and large furniture. "Just the essentials," it says in its old timbre. "Just what you need. No more." But our home doesn't just refuse to house the extras: this 1950s bungalow has designs on our family, too.

There are five of us: Linda and I share the master bedroom, the twins tuck into bunk beds in the back corner bedroom, and our son bunks in the room next to ours. I measure the space around our queen-size bed with my tape measure: I discover there's less than three feet of clearance between it and the wall on any of its sides. No ensuite bathroom. No couch or easy chair, or TV. It's a sleep room.

Once I'm done with sleep, the room presses me out of the space and into the 34-inch hallway. The hallway squeezes me up and out into the one main room of the house—the living room/dining room. While awake, this is the space. And while we're awake we're all here.

Pressed out of bed this Sunday morning, I arrive at the dining room table with this essay and a few musings I want to scribble down. The whole lot of us has suffered the same fate: our home forced us out of our rooms and up the hall. Mom reads the paper at one end of the table. Ezra, our son, carefully arranges a cast of pencil-crayon characters across a page. May, one of the twins, bingo-daubs a page pink. Elise, the other twin, joins me and sits on my knee.

"What are you doing, Dad?" she asks.

"I am writing about our house," I explain.

"Oh," she replies.

Ezra asks me to record a story he'd like to dictate. So I do, while Elise doodles on my pages. And here we sit together, the way our home suggests we should.

The house, like a Jell-O mould, presses us into a lasting shape. And when the mould is removed, the shape wiggles and varies a little, but it's still recognizable. When we leave our bungalow and visit a larger home—to visit friends, for instance—our children will often hang around with the adults, playing in tight around us, as if we still were in our own home.

It's pretty difficult to store or hide any personal baggage. The house has no place for it. I can't hide joy, sorrow, or anger from any of them nor they from me. So we have issues. Daily. And we deal with the difficulties that come up moment-by-moment: we must if we are to live in this house. And we need to interact because the main space is constantly negotiated: all decisions impinge on everyone in this space. Our home builds close, intimate relationships and an in-your-face approach to problem solving.

Although often difficult to live with, I find the bungalow's stoicism is the wood of good living for our times. This house frames us with its own idea of family and simplicity: it shapes how we approach material goods, how we feel toward one another, how we experience one another and, most profoundly, the way we define ourselves: we're set in cement, piped and plumbed, wired, taped and floored.

We naively bought this bungalow thinking we'd move into it.

It turns out, in fact, the bungalow moved into us.

Originally published in the Globe and Mail, Facts & Arguments,
January 11, 2002.

4

SHORT ANSWERS TO TALL QUESTIONS

U
P THE GRAVEL ROAD we walk, the usual dust hammered to the ground by a pounding rain from the night before. The humidity clouds around as we walk, slicking our skin. On either side of the road, canola burns day-glow yellow against the morning blue sky.

My three-year-old daughter walks as though she's alone. She concentrates on something that I'm not aware of, and her concentration makes me invisible. She stops and examines the road, the way a doctor eyes a patient. May ambles from shoulder to shoulder, studying the ground. I linger behind. She's studying the dirt and stone, reading the pathology of a dirt road in southeast Saskatchewan. I'm looking at her.

As I watch her read the road, I wonder, as I do most days, what she's doing. But I've learned enough to know I should be quiet. Her madness has method, I know. For her, life is no question: it's an intuitive response to her world.

Now she's looking for something. She works her way up along the ditch, and plucks something from a soft pit on the road's shoulder.

"This one," she says with certainty.

She looks at her find and smiles to herself, then begins to skip up the road. The worn-down noses of her pink sneakers dip, skip after skip, into the damp black dirt. She stops suddenly, doubles over and digs something out of the road—another rock, I think.

"This one. It's just a baby one," she says in a small, singsong voice.

Questions have a use, but speaking as a man who makes his living asking questions, they get tiring: questions demand work. When a question captures my mind, weariness enters my body. I need to work to bring resolution. And my mind will not stop asking questions. I have a lot of work to do.

Questions recognize a lack of knowledge. When we question, we lack. If we lack, we must get. Questions generate the hum of desire that drives us through the long years of living. As I walk this road, my mind fills itself with thoughts of better things—dreams of answers to questions. Not May, though.

What she is doing, I've never seen her do before. It's her first time. But her action looks practised and natural. I recognize only the look in her eye. She's certain. She's never been to this place, I know. She hasn't even been to a place like it. For that matter, we haven't even gone for a walk on a dirt road before, she and I.

Answers bring rest. Answers soothe the sting of the question: the question's work is complete. Most of the time, I don't get answers. To live without neurosis, I must forget all the questions I have on my mind. There are many ways to forget. But May isn't bothered by questions. Not yet.

Answers bring a state of completeness. If questions drive us to eat, to consume, answers are a signal that we are full, whole; nothing more is necessary. May is not on this walk for the same reason I am. I walk because I'm hungry for answers; she walks because she is full.

She moves a couple of measured steps towards the road's side and digs her index finger underneath another stone. "This is the mommy one," she whispers. She cradles them in her palm and gently rolls her latest find into her other hand. I hear the soft click as the three stones knock together. Their sound marked the first time those stones had met: another small first in the universe.

I, the rational one, know her confidence is not a plausible position. What could she possibly imagine she's doing? How can she be so sure? What kind of knowledge does she have and where does it come from? My puzzlement does nothing to infect her confidence. Perhaps that's why she turns me invisible with the force of her concentration.

Now she walks and stares at the chattering rocks in her hand, muttering something motherly and instructive to them. Brown hair streaked blonde from the summer sun flops around her berry-brown shoulders. Her purple sundress sashays around her.

The Earth's spine bones up underneath the dirt road as we walk on. She steps quietly, half-singing a song she knows. Then suddenly she halts and the last half-notes leave. She spies an earthy scar on the raised bone between the ruts. The stones rattle as she rolls them from her fingers into the blemish. She nudges each stone into place and thumbs each into the soft, rain-moistened dirt.

"They're home," she announces absently.

A breeze gusts, then stillness—a cosmic sigh. The road stretches and sags before us. In the first breath after her ministrations, I reappear in her world and she runs to me for a hug.

Afterwards, I get a hint of what might have happened and who she is. Like a typical parent, I'm never sure. She is as certain as stone. Life seems backward at this moment: it begins with answers and ends in questions. Although answers, through time and doubt, erode into questions.

And this is the difference between May and me this day. I live life as a question—she lives it as an answer.

Originally published in the Globe and Mail, Facts & Arguments,
March 28, 2002.

5

PICKING SLIM

OUR FIRST FAMILY PET needed a name. Linda presents the kids with an unnamed fish. "Do you want to name it?" she asks. The kids glance up from their play at the fish. No huddle or consultation. Without a blink, one of them replies, "His name is Slim." The others instantly agree and return to play. I was hoping for something more considered. A name is the fragrance of fate. But the stick-and-stone is this: he is Slim.

As a parent I'm especially sensitive to names. My five-year-old son is in his sister's bedroom. I can hear him talking like a salesman. "I'll give you one of my chocolates if you get on my elevator," he says. The girls must be uninterested in his offer because he repeats it several times. Knowing a little about boys, and how willingly they part with candy, I was drawn down the hallway. I entered the room. Elise, one of his twin sisters, is poised on the edge of the top bunk, considering stepping onto the elevator.

"That is not an elevator," I cried. "That's two bathrobe belts and a doll mattress." I could tell from the cloudy look in the girls' eyes, I had not succeeded in turning the elevator back into its original form. "That is NOT an elevator," I said firmly, as Elise dangled a toe tentatively and contemplated shifting her weight. I tried again. "It-is-two-bathrobe-belts-and-a-doll-mattress." The emphasis and slow delivery stick. I see Elise blink and her foot moves back to the edge of the bunk bed. My son is disgusted with my intervention. He's angry that I worked so hard to turn his imaginative work into something as banal as two bathrobe belts and a doll mattress.

The name-calling continues over lunch. "That's not an airplane," I complain. "That's a cracker." This is the power of naming: implied in each name are the rules of how that thing must be treated and its eventual fate. Name-calling is an argument of consequence: if a cracker is really an airplane and the pilot is a "maniac"—as my son suggests—then it makes perfect sense that the cracker careens into the wall and disintegrates on the floor, cargo and all: it's the inevitable result. But if I can turn the airplane into a cracker before the crash, the fate changes, and suddenly the only sensible thing is to eat it—at the table.

This is the war in our house: it is the war of names. We battle over what should a thing be called. These children use names to transform almost any object into anything else: solid, liquid, or gas. My job is to make sure it falls within acceptable tolerances and defend what I believe to be reality.

In the eye of the war sits Slim. His name is secure. Neither his name, nor his security affects him much. Linda calls me over to the fish bowl. Slims drifting listlessly at the bottom of his tank. Together we agree that he is too slim. He needs more food.

Another day, I emerge from a phone conversation to find my daughter playing with babies and dogs in the living room.

She's deep in the atmosphere of play and, at the moment, the dogs and babies are conversing happily in tiny tones. She cradled a baby in her arms, although the baby looked as though it had spit up. "Those are not dogs and babies," I say. "Those are your glitter glue bottles and," I added, "they're leaking on the furniture." The miasma lifts, the living room is covered with an entire collection of oozing glitter glue bottles. I run around with water and paper towel daubing away the glue stains. "Bad babies," my daughter grumbles as the gas of imagination leaves her.

Another meal, and I'm renaming something I believe to be fruit. "Those grapes are not bowling balls," I say to two girls who bowl the oblong things down the wood of the table. My renaming efforts fail, and I consider the level of effort required to stop the tournament. I'm tired, so I don't bother trying again. Instead, they get a stern warning after one of them lofts the ball down most of the alley: lofting the ball isn't allowed in a bowling alley, either.

Nothing is safe from the heat of names. The smog of possibility hazes the house. Five minutes ago, it was a castle. Now it's an unspecified variety of plant. Now I see the kids swimming up the hallway: we're in a lake. Their names tear the house down and renovate in seconds, without a permit. Once the kids go to bed and fall asleep, our house is what it ought to be: a bungalow. It's one of the rare moments our house fits into the zoning. For several hours things will remain unchanged, for I have put the magicians to sleep.

Later one night, with the kids asleep, I happened to look in on Slim. His lovely red plumes are drab, folded and grey. I call Linda over. Together we secretly agree the fish is nigh unto death. He's Slim. I throw a few tiny pellets of food into the tank. A last supper, perhaps.

Before we left on a holiday this summer, we took Slim over to a friend's house. Slim is still grey, his body wrinkled like a walnut. Not more than an hour after dropping him off, we get the fateful call: Slim had passed away. The funeral was short, although he was flushed with full honours. His death seemed untimely, so we consulted someone who knew fish well. When we told her Slim's story, the tragic fog cleared: we fed him too much, too often. He ate pellet after pellet—eating himself to death. Slim was our understanding. Slim was our warning. Slim was his life span.

Sticks and stones may break bones, but names are the parcel of destiny.

Originally published as "It's slim pickings when picking Slim" in the Globe and Mail, Facts & Arguments, September 4, 2002.

6

THE REAL REASON SANTA CLAUS LAUGHS

THE WISDOM GOES THIS way: "it is more blessed to give than to receive." I remember hearing that one as a young child, wondering who would fall for that line. I always felt those who clung to that advice were hoping for lots of really large gifts from everyone else. As a parent, I know now that this is not advice but a profound truth.

My relatives have taught me this lesson most pointedly, and repeatedly. All of them have a most pleasant demeanor, very supportive and caring, and they know how to laugh. Yet, their gifts, the gifts they buy for my children reveal a genial diabolism that few understand.

Three Christmases ago an aunt bought our young son 10,000 sticky notes. I remember him strolling around the house with 150 of his collection in hand, looking for interesting places to stick them. And now, three years after the gift hit, I often discover after a stroll through the house, as I did today, that I have one stuck to my sock. The sticky notes were only the first fist in a bamboozling wave of offensives.

The same Christmas a grandma purchased our kids a little plastic guitar that did three hard-rock guitar solos. The real barb of the gift was the volume knob, a lump of twiddlely plastic just below the fake strings. The guitar played the well at a whisper volume, encouraging parents to believe that a child might play with it quietly. The child playing with the toy would push one of the buttons and get the guitar solo going, and then fiddle with the knob. Once the child discovered that the volume was full, he or she was content and left it there. The volume control served only to help the child confirm that, in fact, the screaming plastic was up as loud as it could go. The second row of knuckles finishing a left-right combination.

The attacks continued on regular holiday intervals ever since that fateful Christmas three years ago. Our family suffered a crippling volley two years ago: someone asked our kids if they wanted a free, full drum kit. Someone happened to be giving one away. What adult with a clear head would do such a thing? And what child with a clear mind would say no to drums? I wished vainly that a quiet musical sentiment would prevail. However, any childish sensibility cannot tolerate the quiet playing of drums. Drums are to be beaten senseless with a blizzarding wooden bravado.

At the twin's birthday, last year, another relative socked us with her gift – glitter glue. One of our girls received 40 multi-coloured tubes of glue. The other received 14 large bottles of the stuff. What do you do with litres of glue? You glue things. Paper, to begin with. And when you run out of paper, which is easily done when you think of how much glue is needed to coat an entire sheet of paper, you move on to other, bigger things. Hair. Clothes. Furniture. Children.

Last Christmas brought the last boat to the beachhead: paint. It wasn't the petite pucks of paint, but ten half-litre bottles of poster paint, with easy-pour lids, all ready to go, complete with brushes, rollers and paint stamps, all in an attractive container with a handle on the top. I noted the conspicuous absence of paper with the gift.

So as Christmas approaches, I find myself contemplating defensive strategies to counter this year's hits. I wonder if I should allow our children to open their gifts this year. Perhaps I should unwrap all the kids' gifts the night before Christmas, and replace any contraban with socks. That could take care of the receiving.

This is a year of giving, though. Every gift is an opportunity to return the sentiment of the blessing we have received. For Christmas, I'm imagining a gleeful gift of complete wood burning sets for every young niece and nephew. For birthdays and other special occasions, we'll pepper our relatives' children with canisters of fun slime, sprinkle-top canisters of craft sparkles, spray cans of silly string, hamsters and fish that sing endless, pointless songs, stocked with the best batteries money can buy. When they come over to visit, we'll send them home with the stuff — our unspoken, smiling revenge.

Yes, it is more blessed to give than receive. And this is not an endorsement of selflessness; this wisdom disguises a military secret, and a first principle of sound battle strategy. Here is the truth: receiving does much more damage than giving. In sport terms, the best defense is a good offence. So my credo this Christmas, more than any other, is to indulge in the joy of giving. For the joy of giving is all that can temper the good grief of getting.

Originally published in the Globe and Mail, Facts & Arguments, November 27, 2002.

7

ODE TO THE TICK TOCK ROUNDY

THE WHOLE RITUAL BEGINS with the school bell.

At the belch of the bell, children spill through the school's doors and into the playground. Each child commandeers a piece of idle playground equipment, if he or she happens to be the first to arrive. The child shouts orders to any following children who enlist by showing interest in that particular equipment.

Parents slowly arrive and take up posts circling the playground, while probably 100 children swarm over the equipment like ants on a doughnut.

Parents begin the duty of surveillance, slinging forsaken school wares over arms and shoulders while casually conversing with parents nearby. Some of the parents sport a hot beverage, which they sip while on duty.

The parents ignore the world of the playground, remaining in the orbits of conversation looping the playground.

The children ignore the buzzing circle of parents in favour of the playground's whirling nucleus.

The worlds of the parent and child only meet in ruptures between the two worlds: casual transcendence, familial fission.

When a child falls wounded, the parent passes his or her coffee to a conversation partner and sets down dangling school accoutrements and attends to the fallen. Where light damage is sustained, the circle of parents often bends inward to follow the attending parent into the playground to maintain conversation until the circle can regain its shape.

In cases where a child's wounds are dire, the parent must sever conversation and directly address the child's distress. In these cases, the circle of parents does not bend inward, but permits the attending parent to enter the playground to do his or her work.

Occasionally a parent will forsake conversation to play with the children. If a parent enters that world, and if his or her contribution is deemed significant enough by the children, he or she becomes temporarily immortalized.

A while ago, for instance, a dad broke away from the ring and began removing the shoes of children who came down the slide, flinging those shoes as far as he could into the field.

He was rewarded by the children with a name for his game, with which he would be hunted and haunted by children everywhere: The Shoe Game.

They would approach him directly with the question: "Can you play The Shoe Game?" If he would not respond favourably, that child would sometimes approach another parent in the circle with the same question: "Would you play The Shoe Game?"

This dad's contribution hardened into a concept and an identity as solid as playground pebble and tin, instantly understood whenever a child used the words "The Shoe Game."

Not only did the game become a name, but the game's name stuck to this plucky dad. The kids called him "The Shoe Game Guy" or more politely as "The Shoe Game Dad." His real name is not known to the children, nor is it known to me. He skyrocketed from anonymity to an identity defined entirely by the children.

On the far side of the playground there are two tire swings. The tire swings are in ceaseless motion while one, two or three kids, sometimes hordes, clump and swing on the two, fairly new steel-belted radial tires hanging from chains.

This is one portion of the playground where children will sometimes summon parents as a source of energy to push the tires. If a parent responds to the call from the tire swings, one side of the circle of parents often flattens into a line as one or two parents step up to keep parents in conversation, while pushing.

My favourite bench sits sideways to the late noon sun on the bottom end of the playground near the tire swings.

I confess that The Shoe Game was too much of a commitment for me. I preferred smaller investments in the playground world. Like other parents, I am often called on to push the tire swing.

I do not always answer this call since I believe tire-swing pushing is somewhat of an art and hence requires an effort that must be sparingly offered. When I do respond, I offer a limited number of pushing sessions so the quality of my art remains high.

These pushing sessions have slowly been gaining a reputation, and some children began to request my pushing favours.

Sometimes I refuse, sometimes I give in, depending on my resources. Robin, a friend of our family, one day named my variation of tire-swing push. And I returned subsequent days to find that same name still in use: an invocation, an invitation, a name. My name.

Let me tell you my reward, the syllabled treasure that rolls now in my mouth like candy.

Sweet with precision, hardened by temporary immortality, smooth with today's familiarity.

I am brought into their world and made real with this name:

Tick Tock Roundy.

Originally published in the Globe and Mail, Facts & Arguments,
January 10, 2003.

8

OF MOUNTAINS, MOONS, WHALES, AND JUNE

I AM STANDING WITH MY children, who are staring at a mountain rising before our feet. The children babble and shriek as they meet the mountain. Their responses slop on the mountain like paint. We don't get up to the mountains as often as we should. I've seen the mountain many, many times before. I know what mountains are. I even know how they got here. I don't even look up. I don't need to look any more. "Look at that, Dad," one daughter says to me. I look for her sake, knowing what I'll see.

I am standing at the foot of a mountain. "Who built that?" says my young son. He is hunting a thought big enough to fit what he sees. I tell him that it wasn't built by any person: It's a mountain. My poor answer leads to his next question: "What's a mountain?"

My dictionary calls a mountain "a large, abrupt, natural elevation of the ground." I find myself nodding as I read it. It makes sense. It is reasonable. One sentence in an official publication and the question is put to bed. It need not be asked again. But as I stand at the foot of the mountain, I realize that this answer is not adequate. I start a few sentences, but the words quit before they're out. I look at the mountain again. It looms, now. Wonder makes the mountain too big for thought. Reason shrinks it enough to fit easily. How big is this mountain supposed to be?

I console myself: Reason is a popular corruption. One of its larger flaws is that it is far too easily satisfied. Reason only works if the senses have been numbed enough to the presence of this ponderous mound of rock, that a definition, a tiny one-liner, could possibly cover this thing. It's an attempt to paint a red barn with a pint of green paint. It's a trade: the mountain for a molehill.

My son listens to my definition of a mountain politely, but then five minutes later he asks the same question. He repeats his question because he assumed I could answer in proportion and kind to his question. He expected a mountain-sized answer. And I repeat my answer, as though it ought to answer his question. The danger of my answers is plain enough: He might come to believe they are adequate. My answers bully his questions into silence. If my answers win, I have helped him to dress his wonder with a Nixon mask.

My children are much more reasonable than I am. My daughter holds the giant sucker she purchased. "Look what I buyed," she brags to her brother.

"Look what you bought, dear," said I, to correct her. "But, Dad," she protested, "I knowed how to say it." And, she's right.

Technically, she applies the rules of speech too consistently, more consistently than I do. My big job, now, is to short-circuit her reason with the many, many exceptions of language. Oddly enough, I have learned to think of these exceptions to the language's logic as reasonable.

My children's questions help me map my vast and sprawling ignorance. Late in June, my daughter May watches the horizon slide an oatmeal-raisin moon into the sky. "What is the moon?" she asks. I am tempted to tell her it's a natural satellite of the Earth, orbiting it monthly, illuminated by the sun and reflecting some light to the Earth. She would take a moment to measure my answer against what she has seen with her eyes. Then, she would look at me as though I had told her a joke that she doesn't understand. Instead, I shut my mouth, and let her moon hang there.

Yes, my children are more reasonable than I. Listen to this question my daughter, Elise, asked: "Why aren't the planets noses?" She had to ask it several times, until I understood the question's size. I couldn't find an answer big enough. Why aren't the planets noses? Why aren't horses as small as dogs and dogs as big as whales? Why don't birds fly in the water and fish swim in the air?

Honey, I must shrink the truth. I must if my puny answers are to work. Ahem, ahem: The professor in me clears his throat, preparing to deliver a short lecture on the physical characteristics of these animals and their habitats. After dismissing the first question as just plain silly, the essence of the lecture would be this: Horses are as big as horses because they're horses, dear. Dogs are dogs, and whales are whales so their size is just right for who they are, you see? Water is water-like and fish are fish-like so the two must go together; birds are bird-like, and thus, cannot fly in water, which is not air-like. If I offered the lecture in a condescending tone,

I could encourage her to take note. Instead, her reasonable questions dwarf my answers and bully reason into wonder.

Here is what my children ask of me: Let us be reasonable, they say. Let us gawk at the beauty of what we do not know. Let our best questions help us see a world that exceeds our answers. Let mountains be mountains and the moon be the moon, whales be whales, and June be June. Let our jaws hang slack at this impossible universe, the outrage of life, and wonder at ourselves and how we ever woke up.

Originally published as "Whales are whales so their size is right" in the Globe and Mail, Facts & Arguments, June 3, 2003.

9

AN ELEGY FOR THE WEEDED GOD

THE THREE HUDDLED AND began to report and account for new facts in each of the preternatural beings holding sway over the children's minds: they meet to tend their garden of gods. This is not the first meeting of its kind. Our three children, since they are close in age, meet like this at several points over the year, ready to weed or feed the gods they keep. First item on today's agenda: the Easter Bunny.

"I think it's not a bunny, it's a person," my son declares. His sisters are delighted by his theory, but need the proof.

"Why do you think that?" asks May.

"If it was a bunny, then it would eat all the chocolate, and throw out the black jelly beans."

He's hit on a bit of solid logic, here. His sisters agree, pleased by the progress of collective thought, their theories expanding with the universe.

May chases down one of her own suspicions. "Dad, did you make the Easter Egg Hunt?"

Typically in these situations, I try neither to confirm nor deny anything.

"Why would you think that, dear?" I reply. Since the meeting is being held in our mini-van, and I'm driving, I change my focus to the traffic for a moment to dodge her question.

The meeting finishes with a short discussion of our home's chimney and the likelihood of someone fat sucking it in for the length of the cinderblock stack. And where, precisely, he would get out, should such an event occur.

Together they conclude that it's more likely that he should come through the door. The problem, Elise puts succinctly: If he lands on the roof, how would he get down to the door? A ladder, the other two guess, but from the dissatisfied silence, I can tell this discussion isn't through.

Last year, at a meeting much like this, the tooth fairy was tethered and tested out of existence. Torn out by the root. I overheard that meeting, too. The doubt arose as it was discovered that the tooth fairy left a hefty 10 bucks per tooth at a family friend's house, while she left a mere dollar at our own. The disparity led to a lengthy discussion of the Tooth Fairy's person. The children theorized over the potential motives of the tooth fairy, borrowing heavily from their own theology of Santa Claus. Perhaps it was this other child's goodness, based on foreknowledge or an accrued goodness that was unknown to us: these gods, after all, share an omniscience. Or, perhaps the tooth fairy does not know how to count very well. This was merely speculation of course. The discussion moved to a more stable footing.

One incontrovertible virtue of all preternatural beings, intuited by my children, is that of equality: all of these idols must be fair, since they deal with all children. The nest of syllogisms went something like this:

1. The friend gets 10 bucks for each of his teeth.
2. We get one dollar for each of our teeth.
3. That's not fair.
4. All preternatural beings must be fair.
5. Hence, the tooth fairy is incompetent or human, and, given the facts, isn't worth the belief.

The conclusion was firm enough for the three of them that they embarked on some fact-finding interviews with Linda (my spouse) and me. In the school community, they found those who would support such a radical doubt. Armed with their own findings, corroborated by the findings of others, they attacked us with pointed questions at a time when it was not possible to duck the slap of their doubt. After a short discussion, they left the tooth fairy behind, never to return.

I'm not so ready to let go of tooth fairy this time. They leave her corpse behind, but I get my chance to say goodbye to her properly. I left her in a hurry too, many years ago, forgetting my farewell. I gaze on her carefully, pay my respects, and catch up to my kids.

From what I understand from other parents, the tooth fairy is always one of the first to go. Something unbelievable about her I guess, her figure too slight to hold her heavenly seat. She seems much like one of those new-faced actors serving on the Star Trek crew. Slightly loveable, yet entirely expendable. A training wheel on the bicycle of belief. As I watch them tend to their remaining gods today, I wonder which ones will dig in and grow and which will compost with the leavings of childhood.

The bunny's next on the block, I believe. Although questions surround the entry and exit of Santa, his essential character is unchallenged. So far.

He may watch my children's behaviour, but I think the children keep a fatter file, and he has more to lose, should the deal go bad. Up the ladder they go, knocking away a god at every rung.

These little theologians, miniature philosophers, make this kind of speculation seem natural, easy. They hum and haw, sometimes rub a hairless chin, drawing on their own observations and experiments, assaulting their own belief with their own science. Somehow, they've guessed that all beliefs are not equal. They've also decided that a belief must stand up to their own reckoning of the universe. If it doesn't, it must go. They pull each of their idols between each being's claims and the soil of their own life and living.

Not many gods can withstand the stretch.

Originally published in the Globe and Mail, Facts & Arguments,
September 30, 2003.

10

SANTA GIVETH, BUT ANTI CLAUS TAKETH AWAY

S ANTA CLAUS HAS A long-lost ne'er-do-well brother. His sibling is as much of a thief as Santa is generous.

The problem with Santa is that the volume of goods he and others bring to our home exceeds those leaving the house. The influx whittles a sharp point on the law of material goods: That which has been given must be taken away; that which has come must go. Ownership is always temporary. The law of material goods creates a practical problem in our home: Who gets rid of things?

Though there is no champion of disposal, the volume of things we own demands something be done. The Grinch would be an excellent candidate for the job, except he recanted and returned the Christmas he stole. But he clearly understood the Christmas Problem.

Consumption creates the need for disposal. Dr. Jekyll and Mr. Hyde: The fat philanthropist demands a thieving recycler of equal heft. The job description is clear, but it has no title. So, let me name this role. If Santa Claus is all about bringing gifts, the yang to his yin is Anti Claus, the remover of things. Since I play the favoured Santy, I also play the evil Anti.

Bringing new things into the house is almost always done with pomp and pageantry. There's a party, or some kind of celebration, or the sting and zing of a new purchase. There are people in chimneys, rabbits with baskets, ghosts and witches, fairies, clowns, cakes and candles, parades and pictures. We dedicate entire days to the celebration of things coming into our home. But the disposal is solitary and silent. It is a ritual too, but one practised, in our house, in a shroud of silence, in utter secrecy.

I sneak now, because my overt Anti Claus efforts entirely failed. Once, when I finished culling the toy collection, I showed the kids what I thought we could get rid of. As they looked in the bag they rediscover each as though it were a hundred dollar bill. I put the empty bag away. Now I don't consult, I creep.

Today the wide mouth of each child's toy box is swollen beyond capacity. They get widgets for sitting still in their chairs at school; gidgets from the dentist for sitting still in his chair; gadgets from restaurants for sitting still in their chairs; prizes from cereal boxes and candy; trinkets from baby sitters; hand-me-downs from older kids, and of course, the regular influx at birthdays and holidays.

I steal into the girls' room first and paw through the heaps of toys with the coldness of a crooked accountant. I pilfer the toys from the bottom of the toy chests. All the things I found on the bottom layer of the toy boxes go into my bag. I check my watch: not much time. Plastic puppies, smiling hamburgers, whirling dancing girls with overwound springs, bulbous heads of cartoon heroes on wheels, plastic "collector" drink cups, headless Barbies, cars jammed with PlayDo, wingless planes, horses with nodding heads, and a salad of unintelligible toy bits.

My grocery bag fills quickly and I haven't even finished the first toy box. I get a garbage bag, and finish the second toy box. I need two hands to carry the sack of plunder as I head into my son's room.

I cull his toy box and the bag strains as I head downstairs for my sweep of basement playthings. By the time I finish the basement toy boxes, the bag can no longer handle the weight. A lumpy patch of the black plastic greys as it weakens. I drop the bag as the grey bulge thins into a hole, smiles and yawns, burping a few toys onto the floor. I dump all the toys into a new bag and then double-bag it for extra reinforcement. Then I drag my loot out to the garage, to a spot where no one would see it, and I wait.

I watched the kids play over the next few days. No one noticed the missing swag, so I shored up my confidence and put out the 43-pound sack (yes, I weighed it) of toys.

My sneak ritual has evolved into a full-time undercover op. Though Santa gets all the glory, I've come to realize that he needs his lesser brother. My sneaks balance the Christmas Problem. My dirty deeds give the stout saint the space to work his magic.

Originally published in the Globe and Mail, Facts & Arguments,
December 5, 2003.

11

JULIE'S PORTRAIT

THE PICTURE ABOVE THE preacher is wrong. All wrong. It is a stained-glass window, lit from behind by a buzzing fluorescent bulb. Each of the glass shapes is a solid block of colour. The scene spends eight different colours to portray a path leading to the foot of the cross.

Below the window, on two roman columns, sits a small white box adorned with bunches of white lace and, on top, a modest bouquet of flowers. It's a coffin. And inside lies a six-week-old baby girl I'll call Julie. The lace, in the light of the church, hides uncounted shades of grey. The flower petals downplay hundreds of shades of pink, appearing as though they're all one.

The funeral begins and the candle-lighter approaches the candle and holds a lit match to the wick. She nudges the wick and backs away, but the light doesn't hold. She steps forward and nudges it again; and, again, one last time, before the flame takes to the wick.

The preacher's message is the only acceptable one under these circumstances. He affirms God's goodness, his absolute undying love for all of humanity. With eloquence he points to an evident grace. Yet, his own pain, and the pain of those in the room, goads him to acknowledge that it doesn't seem right that this girl should die, that she should be lying in a white box in front of us all. He cannot, dare not say she is an exception to that grace, and rightly so, for he cannot know. Perhaps this is one of grace's unrecognized hues. This, too, is terrifying, unspeakable.

At the interment, the pallbearers bear this little girl down a grim row of headstones in the snow. Snow-covered little toy bears and bunnies litter the ground. One headstone marked the rest of a two-year-old boy named Mat. The whole family had written their Christmas wishes on signs and stuck them around the headstone. Another stone marks a set of twins who didn't make it. Polaroid photographs half-buried in the snow next to mud-smudged granite. At the end of the row, on a grass-coloured rug covering the mud of the freshly dug grave, now sits this little white box. In this light, its colour has changed. Shadows hide in new folds of fabric. The pink rose petals bleach under the white winter sun.

The service ends and the preacher leaves us wallowing in irony: We cannot pray a little, loved life into this world with any certainty. Nor can we beat the bad out. This is mystery. This is life.

Of the extended family of this little girl, most are artists. One resurrects her little life in image on the funeral's pro-gram cover. Another recreates a tender moment between mother and daughter with her pencil on paper. The little girl's aunt resurrects this little girl in word, prolonging sev-eral moments of her life for as long as her words shall last.

A pianist, with Handel, makes notes of her life. Each uses art to resuscitate her. Sometimes art renders the world restored. We resurrect her with art to do what God would not.

Art that doesn't restore the world must at least be truthful. An eight-tone picture in stained glass doesn't restore the world and its bigger fault is that it doesn't tell the truth. The fault lies not with the subject matter—the cross works—the problem is in the art. The one-tone blue sky, with the one-tone white clouds surround the top part of a one-dimensional, uniformly toned brown cross. The grass is green. The path is light brown, and as the path narrows approaching the base of the cross, the brown darkens by a shade.

The light from behind erases any shadow. The measured glass shapes all meet in smooth joins at every edge.

What I need is a rock. I need a rock to make that picture window speak the truth. I would begin by throwing that rock through the glass. Smash out each pane. Once the picture was out, I'd smash the light behind it, for it helped that picture lie. And then I'd replace it with something that tells the truth: Julie's portrait.

It would be a painting where the colours run together. It would be red like the corners of weeping eyes. Black as a finished death. Yellow and sick with home and hope. Purple with desire. Frail-bone blue. White laughter.

All colour mingled. Fractal figures spooning over a once-white canvas. It would be a painting where a person might see a cross or not depending on how one looks at it.

A painting where those who see a cross and move their gaze away from the painting struggle to find that hope again when their eyes return. All of it brought to the eye with ambient light. Lumpy paint soaked in light and shadow, some brushed, some poured, some thrown, some knifed onto the

canvas. Paint oozing from the picture onto the wall, drip-
ping and drying on the carpet below.

There it would hang, nailed to wood, a transcendent,
frantic, mad choir of colour: rich, violent, infinite; singing
everything and its opposite at once.

In a glance, one would see truth: life is a bloody, beautiful
mess.

The first and last elements of living, birth and death,
create a gap that we live between, big enough for almost everyone; only good art can make sense of it.

Originally published as "Honest art presents life's truths at a
glance" in the Globe and Mail, Facts & Arguments, February 10,
2004.

1 2

CASHIERED CONFESSIONS

W E'D READ THE ADVERTISEMENT in the paper, and were completely prepared. A church at the end of our street was hosting a large garage sale, so we walked the long way around the block. A crowd crushed into the back of the church, flush and fevered because they were the first to paw the tables of tarnished treasure. All three of my children disappeared into the din, headed straight to the toy section. I browsed the hardware and chose an excellent light fixture and a few tools, and then joined the kids. We paid our money and carried our plunder out the door. Cash first, then carry.

Exalted, the kids and I left with our armloads, and headed for home, using a short cut that would take us right past the front of the church. As we rounded the corner, the doors sprang open. I was expecting a parishioner in dungarees. Instead, two somber looking men, in matching suits, held the doors wide open.

All four of us were surprised. Me, grubby and bed-head-ed, with my light fixture and tools; Ezra with his massive pump-action squirt gun; May and a plastic doll castle; Elise and her new toy dog, to which she'd attached a real dog collar and matching leash. The two men didn't even notice us. We waited, curious as to what we'd stumbled across.

A few moments later, several staggering pallbearers ported a gleaming coffin through the open doors. I shushed the kids and hurried them to the other side of the street as the pallbearers seesawed the casket down the steps. "It's a funeral," I whispered. The pallbearers hefted the polished box into the back of the hearse across the street from where we stood. "Is there really a body in there?" one of my kids asked.

I looked at the things in my arms. I looked at the things in our hands and wondered if—surely not—the items had belonged to the dead person. A funeral and a garage sale at the same time, each one operating out of the opposite end of the same church. Just coincidence, I supposed. But what an idea! A garage sale and funeral, one magnificent clearance—body and baggage—in one two-pronged everything-must-go ritual, priest presiding over one checkout and the cashier at the other. As I watched the procession leave, the overlap of the morning's events made it easy to see them as ecclesiastical equivalents. The funeral, of course, I recognize as a rite, but what of the garage sale?

There is a certain kind of connection I have with the things I own, a connection between my possessions and the size and feel of the soul. It's as if everything I own curdles, clots and coalesces on my spirit. When I own too much, and the wrong things, my essence seems bulky, thick-fingered and earthbound.

When I rid myself of some of it, some of the worst of it, I feel lighter, and the spirit's buoyancy returns. The hosting of a garage sale seems somehow spiritual.

So, I prepare myself for this spring's garage-sale rite. In this material reconciliation, I search through my belongings, looking for my blunders. I find hoards of venial possessions—those acquired without a forethoughtful malice. There are books I did judge by their covers, but which fell short within them. The silvered promise of several CD's that turned out to be little more than musical ketchup. A brass bed that should have lasted much longer that it did. The many mugs that seemed to have migrated to our cupboards from lands afar. Those, I can bear to look at, for they are my accidental acquirements. I can let go of them with a smile, for I'm able to dismiss their arrival with some suitable justification of accident.

But then, there are my mortal sins. Where, in a purchase frenzy, I have boldly chosen to purchase when it was clearly not wise to do so. Brazen buys done to satisfy other inclinations than those that were best. There are the books I purchased in order that they be seen in my hand and on the shelf. There was a new DVD player I purchased to match the hand-me-down TV. The Playstation I purchased "for the kids."

Several unnecessary tools. Manly amounts of overpurchased hardware. Then, my acquirements by scandalous means: purchases, where I'm certain the wrong price tag was on the item; things "borrowed" from neighbours from years ago and never returned; a vacuum I wouldn't buy from my neighbour's garage sale, but later took out of his garbage can because it was then "free."

I choose from among these things the sins I'm willing to renounce, and arrange them on tables and the floor in the garage. I prepare a parade of substance abuse, and invite the neighbourhood to view material sins. It's an exhibition of my mistakes, brokenness and malice. This garage sale is my public, material confession.

This year's sale will be easier than our first one, last year. On our first garage sale, I was embarrassed to let others into our garage. Surely people would laugh at this foolishness, I thought. I put on my best brave face and opened the garage door and invited the world in to view my wrongdoing. They came inside. They came in droves, in flocks, in herds. And they did not judge me. Instead, they purchased.

Originally published as "Garage sale: used blunders, old sins" in the Globe and Mail, Facts & Arguments, April 29, 2004.

13

HOW TO GET THAT HOLIDAY FEELING

IN THE OLD DAYS, we used to take expensive, travelling holidays. My wife Linda and I used to pop away for a couple of weeks or the odd weekend to the mountains, to the lake, or some exotic place.

The good parts of being away, even for a short time, are well known: one forsakes the whip of work; the waves of phone calls break on the answering-machine tape—and we indulge in activity, food, and drink. On vacation away from home, I soak my psyche in the unfamiliar and the extravagant. And this is the point, I suppose: The vacation of the body becomes a holiday of thought.

Holidays are only meant to help my brain find its way to the beach. I coddle my body to give rest to my mind. And this is travel's particular power: a new setting has a natural power to convince me I have experienced a vacation. The long distances I've travelled, sometimes halfway around the world, give my brain the sense that it has been properly rested, that it has been on vacation.

On one of my favourite holidays, I took my body to California, and parked it on Pismo Beach. I told friends before I left I was heading to California and they confirmed what I was trying to believe myself: I was going to a wonderful place for a wonderful vacation. The tour brochures assured me that I would experience the "ultimate" retreat. Once my body was there, I waited for my brain to catch up with my body. I relaxed, and promptly, my mind spread out a towel and joined me there, and my vacation began.

Recently, I've experienced the long and unexotic holiday, the gift of time at home, rather than a jet-jaunt to an exotic location—and I can barely cope. Here's a sample of the unexotic home holiday: I muck about the house, and fume for a few minutes in a beach chair in the back yard, attempting to get that vacation feeling. I know I ought to be working on a fence, but I'm on holiday. So, I choose the beach-chair-in-sun instead, and back the chair against the fence, to obstruct the fence's call for attention.

For a moment, I'm content. Then my own thoughts, those sand-kicking beach bullies, arrive. Could I be spending my time more effectively? How could sitting in a chair be considered the right thing to do—ever? Should I be wearing a Speedo with dress socks and shoes?

The phone rings. I'm not going to answer it: I'm on vacation. But who could it be? Should I build a fence in a Speedo? What would the neighbours think? Is there a brochure that could confirm for me that I am having an ultimate moment here? After all, I am not at work, and sitting in a beach chair in my Speedo in my back yard is better than a regular work moment, right?

I pick up the phone and wonder who I could call and brag to them that I am not working today. Maybe I'll call a few people at work, and they can tell me how jealous they are that they are not sitting in a beach chair in my backyard, although I notice, suddenly, that my thighs are sticking to the plastic of the beach chair, which could never be ultimate. Then I realize I'm stupid. I must be, because I'm on holiday and I can't tease the holiday into my mind.

I contemplate running through the sprinkler. Then I wonder if I should wonder if I'm spending my time well. I get tired of my thoughts, and go for a run. And as I'm running, I realize that I exercise almost every day of my life. Shouldn't I be taking a break? Then, depression: I am certain the holiday is going to end and I won't have been able to push, pull, or drag a beach chair and bathing suit into my brain.

The travelling holidays I used to take gave me an extrinsic holiday feeling. I only had to open my eyes in the morning, and the unfamiliar place confirmed my vacation. Travel also neuters any urge to be productive. On a beach, I can't reach my tools, call my friends, answer the phone, mow my lawn, or pet the dog.

But when I'm at home and I open my eyes in the morning, there is no beach, no sea breeze, no room service to clarify how I ought to feel. So, I let my home repairs and to-do lists overwhelm my days. I work around the house and read heavy, stiff books because it seemed a good use of time. I squander time and sunshine by forcing some fuddled sense of what the holiday ought to be on to an otherwise perfectly good day.

After wrecking five and most of a sixth vacation, I am marginally better at this type of holiday. I shortened my to-do lists enough that it seemed easy to finish. I've made peace with the undone-ness and permanent incompleteness in which I live my life. I gave up attempts to create ultimate vacation moments.

In sum, I made peace with myself and my circumstances. Instead of expecting my vacation to move my mind to the beach, I moved my mind to the beach, and the vacation began. Today is the first day of this year's vacation. I sit very still as I write, and urge my mind toward its own beach. Billions of thoughts threaten to join me here to destroy my vacation. I let them through, let them fall like grains of sand around my feet. I plant my beach chair on top of them all, don my Speedo, and, voilà, I am on holiday.

Originally published in the Globe and Mail, Facts & Arguments,
July 26, 2004.

14

THE DAY A BICYCLE SPOKE

I was running with my daughter, as she, terrified, held the handlebars of her two-wheeler. She wasn't sure, like most, whether she even wanted to try. In the middle of her sixth year of life, she asked me to remove the training wheels of her bike. As I unbolted her training wheels, she bit her lip, asking earnestly how one comes to ride a bike. I answered the way Kierkegaard would have: "I don't know," I said. And it's true. I don't. Riding a bike is a bit of knowledge, like many of the best knowledges we have, that requires that everyone find his or her own way. Words won't work.

She wants me to give her a sure method so she peppers me with questions. I reply with instructional platitudes to try and calm her. She wants bike riding to make sense before she begins. But there is nothing to do but put her on the bike. Balance awakens when she acts as if it exists.

She presses for instruction. I reply by telling her it's going to be fine. She's absolutely frustrated with my confidence that it will go well, because I haven't given her any explanation. My optimism seems unfounded. She wants to be taught. Why won't I teach her? I won't teach her because I can't. There's nothing to be said. Yet, she wants something more than handlebars and a shove.

That anyone learns to ride a bike is a minor miracle. I wonder just how many sleeping capacities are in me. How many have I roused? How many more might I awaken? Can a middle-aged man live every day as though he's learning to ride a bike?

I ignore her intensifying questions and take her up to the field at her school. She's shrieking at her lack of information. She insists she doesn't know what she's doing. I put her on her bike seat and begin to push her up and down the field. The first few times she's deadweight and her weight drops fully into my hands, left then right, as she screeches at me. "This is too hard," she says.

I shrug. "Do you want to learn to ride a bike?" I reply.

"Yes," she says in a way that's meant to wallop me. "But how do you do it?" she asks, venting the anger she's feeling.

"I can't tell you," I said, "because it's sleeping inside you and you have to try until it wakes up." She eyes me suspiciously, as if I might be telling her one of those parental mistruths. She senses that although things aren't square, they're as square as they're going to get.

She lets me hold her shoulders again, and we run up and down the field. This next few runs, she's sitting like a 45-pound egg on the peak of a roof, ready to roll either way at any second. But I notice, as I run, that her front wheel is beginning to steer in the direction she tips.

She's still mad. "You're not helping me, Dad. You're just holding me," she yells. We stop, after her she catches her calf on the sharp face of her pedal. "This is not riding a bicycle. This is boring," she yells through her tears. I give her a minute. She doesn't get off her bike.

"Do you want to learn to ride a bike?" I ask again. She nods, and the tears cut clean paths through her dusty features. I see her agony. I want to help, but the way is silent. "We can do this another day, if you like," I say with a smile. "You don't have to today."

"No," she says and hangs her head.

Up the field we head, and down, up and back again. As we finish the last of the length, she's suddenly light in my hands. I hold her all the way, but she's balancing most of her weight on her own. "You're getting it," I say to her, as we stop.

"This is too hard," she says, "I hate this." She can't feel her progress like I can.

"Do you want to learn to ride?" I ask her again.

She nods sadly. Some odd compulsion drives her on. We go up the field, and when she's more or less balanced, I let go of her briefly. She rides for a few seconds, alone, and I yelp at her success. Her smooth ride wobbles as her consciousness interferes. I grab her shoulders again. At the end of the field she looks at me, frustrated still, and a little bewildered. The next few trips up and back I hold her and release, hold and release, hold and release, hold and release. Her focus slowly rolled inward, into herself.

She stopped commenting at the end of each of our runs. We stopped for a break in silence. She blows dander off a fresh fistful of white-headed weed.

This holding on and letting go seemed like all that I do as a parent. Her weight started out completely in my hands, and I hold on and let go, catch and release. That's all I do. I hold her until she strikes balance; then, I let go.

We begin again. This time, first try, she's flying up the field with me jogging beside her.

She's got it. She's dazed at her success and almost falls. I catch her again. She's up and riding on her own again, and I'm thrilled. I was beside her when it happened. Bike riding is one of those things that she'll never forget.

And so she learned. I rest at the far end of the field while she rides all over the grass, and then begins to teach herself how to start off without me. A few minutes later, she can hardly remember what it was like before she learned how to ride. She's puzzled by her success. "How didn't I know how to do this?" she asks. To her, the big lesson was mastery of two wheels. To me, it was that she abandoned reason and pedalled forward: she gave up understanding in order to learn.

Originally published as "I learn lots from a bike-riding lesson" in the Globe and Mail, Facts & Arguments, May 24, 2005.

15

AMBUSHELS OF APPLES

I WENT OUT THE OTHER day to begin the chore of picking our apple tree's fruit.

On the ground, there were apples everywhere.

I picked my way carefully through them, stepping on a few, extended my ladder and settled it carefully into the tree for my first pick.

The tree stood still in the morning air. It seemed quiet and compliant. The harvest hung thick in the branches. In fact, the branches were loaded. Funny, I hadn't really noticed any of this until I started climbing into the tree.

Suddenly, the tree decided it had something to say to me.

Halfway up the ladder, the tree began to make noises.

Duh, dum, dee-dee-dee-dee, dank, wump. Apples drum-soloing down the garage roof, off the eavestrough, and into the neighbour's yard. Kank. Off the ladder. Thud. Into my picking bucket. Did, Diddy. Off the bucket rim, like practice free throws. Wonk. Into the wheelbarrow below. Wump. On the ground. Tsh, tsh, tsh, wump. Off branches, through leaves to the ground.

Apple rain. Apple hail. Apples in tree crooks. Apples impaled on the pointy parts of my ladder.

I was a target, too. Apples were whacking me on the head and shoulders. I looked up and a big apple whacked my face.

I touched my lip, wondering if I just got my first fat lip from a tree.

I plotted my revenge. I thought applesauce. I thought juice and jelly. I thought pie.

The tree shivered, apples atremble. Apples fell away on their own, or jumped in clumps.

As I stuck my hand into apple bunches, they rolled off my hands, over my hands, down my hands, around my hands. When I trapped one in my hand, two others dropped.

Each bunch required strategic thought. It took me a while to figure out I needed to grab the big ones first, to be sure I didn't lose them.

Some of the apples were bruising each other on the tree as they hung, tangled in swelling knots. The sweet smell of apple filled the air, and brought the wasps, too, so I had to be careful.

An apple fell, hitting a branch, and broke open, sputtering apple pulp and juice all over me.

The apple droplets dried in hard, flawless circles on the lenses of my glasses. The ladder was sticky with apple bits. So were my hands. So were my clothes. My shoes were covered in pulp.

Everything smelled like apples, even things that weren't supposed to, like the dog.

In a tree crook sat an apple. I pulled it up and looked it over, but it was too far gone. There were ants organizing ways of breaking it down and transporting it to the ground below.

I replaced the apple, but the ants were worth a grin.

There must have been 500 apples on the ground but some executive ant picked the apple in the tree crook, and that's what they'll work with.

Bucket by bucket, I cleared the tree. The dog watched me work, but steered clear of the tree's perimeter.

I think the tree informed the dog of its presence, too. On a trip down, I tried to call him under the branches, but he refused, eyeing me with a Newtonian understanding.

I didn't prune the tree last year, and the limbs have stretched impossibly high, holding branches of apples to the sun, like marshmallows held to the celestial fire, like a young schoolgirl's hand stretched skyward with certainty and the rightness of her answer, like a tall child teasing another by holding treasures out of reach. So, I balanced beyond the top of the ladder, between the branches, stretching, twisting, shivering with the tree wood as I reached for the big ones near the top.

When I was done, from our one, small apple tree, there were almost 160 kilograms of apples.

If the apple tree knew how cheap apples were at the grocery store right now, I don't think it would care.

I get the clear impression that this tree has had fun growing these apples, and it's trying to tell me so.

In English class, I was always taught that hyperbole was symbolic and done for effect.

The tree's extravagance was no matter of accident, but a symphonic joy, theme and variation, a dazzling display of capacity, like a young man in a brand new sports car, screaming away from a green light. It's the tree's version of the child's request: "Watch me; watch what I can do."

I took a break and eyed the tree, the dog, my gleanings, and bit into a big, perfect fruit.

The flesh was crisp, the flavour, melodic—no bitter hint of knowledge. Just a bright tang, the taste of everything this tree had to offer, and everything it took to get it.

Originally published as "Apples ambushed me in bushels on picking day" in the Globe and Mail, Facts & Arguments, September 12, 2005.

16

THE CAP GUN WAS LOADED

TO BE HONEST, I never anticipated the moment, as he stood there excitedly in a store, his allowance money shining in one hand, and in the other a brand new cap gun. "Can I get it?" he asked. Behind his words the force of energy equivalent to seven birthday parties.

"Please?"

I reviewed the obvious hurdles. I knew his mother would be slightly disappointed. But through my mind went the moments of my childhood where I would wear my leather holster and, tucked into it, hugging my right hip, was my cap gun. My love of the fine red tape, blotted with the shadowed dots of gunpowder, returned to me. I can remember the hammer falling, the splinters of an orange flame up from the hammer's blow, and the sweet lazy smoke that curled from the barrel and hammer. I remember being fascinated and pulling the trigger time, after time, after time, just studying the spark, the smoke, listening to the different sounds each dot made, reviewing the duds that remained on the cap tape.

As in so many instances the overwhelming nostalgia made me agree that he should get it so I could review with him the experience that had captured his imagination.

So he bought it and brought it home. We took a little heat, him for desiring it, and me for permitting the purchase. But the payoff soon followed: his fascination matched the one I had experienced. I listened to his observations as he ranted about the smoke, the flicker of flame, the sound. How he enjoyed it.

But as boys are wont to do, he asked to take it to school. In my day, it was merely a matter of strapping on the holster and walking to school. These days not so, and, honestly, I had never really considered this potential. "I'm sorry son, but you can't take it to school." He looked at me oddly. "It's not something you'd want to take," I reiterated.

"I can take it in a bag."

"Sorry, son. No."

"I won't play with it until after school."

"Sorry, son. No."

So went the conversation, and I was frustrating him with a staccato "No." Once he was through making a case for method and opportunity to take his gun to school, he switched to motive.

"Why dad? Why can't I take it?" I sighed. And I resisted. But my resistance led to higher levels of frustration until I finally capitulated.

"Because people are afraid of guns," I said.

"Why are they afraid of toys?"

"They're not afraid of toys. But your gun looks real, and guns have done lots of bad things in the world," I replied. This was a bad move on my part. I had "protected" my kids from the news for a long time, because I remember how news sometimes terrified me as a child. But my conversational lead invited an explication in support of my generalization. It was too obvious of a move and he went for it.

"Like what?" I sighed. Maybe he should know the truth. I explained Columbine.

"But dad, it's just a toy."

"I know it's a toy, but other people don't. They might think it's real."

"But I wouldn't do that, Dad."

"I know, son. But others might."

I explained the copycat crime in Taber, Alberta. I explained to him how lockdowns in schools became a practice that grew out of these events. I tried to show him how ideas spread like a virus, as does fear. And that it doesn't matter if there's not another person in the entire world who would do such a thing, nor does it matter whether he would do such a thing, what is real now is the idea that such a thing is possible and its matching fear. The idea and fear, together, constitute a threat and the threat is enough to make a cap gun at school a bad idea. It was a painful lesson into the dark side all connected to this bit of smoking, moulded plastic. In the end, I felt like I'd poisoned him.

His argument to me was about the toy. In essence, he argued, the toy, including the toy gun, is an adult artifact stripped of all its power. This is the essence of his toy cellphone, his collection of spy gadgets, his collection of credit cards, and cars.

But I did not accept his argument, mostly because I had visions of the SWAT team surrounding the school, the red eye of laser gun-sights ranging over the school's brickwork.

Bullhorns, radios, and me being asked to talk him into dropping his gun.

"No," I said. "And that is final."

Oddly enough, instead of being angry with me, he was angry towards his gun. Very angry at it. His constant protest was a personal one: "But, I wouldn't do it, Dad." At the end of the discussion he closed himself in his room and removed the screws from his gun, threatening to smash it and throw it in the garbage. And the response puzzled me, until just now.

I realize that my suggestion that guns were bad had impugned him. He felt guilty for liking something that could represent so much harm to the world. I felt guilty for allowing him to buy it.

And we both came to realize that the cap gun was loaded.

Originally published in the Globe and Mail, Facts & Arguments,
May 23, 2006.

17

PUSHING THE BIG, RED BUTTON

WHENEVER I RODE THE commuter train in Calgary, known as the Light Rapid Transit, I used to enter the train, and immediately turn around to take my place right next to the door. Above each door in most cars was a big, red button. I used to stare at it whenever I rode the Light Rail Transit down town. Underneath there was a sticker that read "Penalty for misuse." Around the button, there was no other instruction, just the warning. Today, as I look at it, I smile.

I smile because once, I sold myself as a photographer. I used to take pictures for minor events, sometimes submit them to a newspaper, and they were sometimes published. For a young hothead, this was the only requirement I needed to call myself a photographer who took photographs (as distinguished from a man who took mere pictures).

One day I happened to sell my services to someone as a photographer. I was invited to photograph a prestigious event by a man who wore bow ties as a matter of routine, part of his artistic shtick. He required a photographer, and would only condescend to a man who took pictures.

I purchased a new camera just for the occasion, a Nikon F2, because in those days, that's what photographers were using. I had a flash with a battery pack slung around my neck, and a T-handle that brought the camera and flash together. I had a few lenses in my hip pack, and almost bought myself an automatic film winder. It did not occur to me that there should be any more to photography than what I had: attitude and equipment.

I arrived at the event, attended by dignitaries from around the world, and began photographing them with my fabulous equipment, with an attitude that was finally justified for I had been recognized at last. Subjects squeezed together, smiled. Made faces at me, toasted me as I let fly spurts of light upon them. I pinched hors d'oeuvres, drank punch, twirled and flashed, my camera and I. I quipped, I courted, I cultured. The bow-tied employer must have been certain he'd hired James Bond now moonlighting as a photographer. Surely I was worthy of a bow tie and ruffles myself. When the speeches were made, who strutted before the audience, posing like a runway model with his Nikon F2? Who checked his hand-held light meter, cursed the dim light, and stroked his philtrum as he puzzled over f-stop with that shutter speed or that one. Who turned to face the audience while he changed his fixed-focal length lenses? The man standing just inside the LRT, staring at the big, red button.

When I took the rolls of film in for development, I picked the best photographic store in the entire city. The price needed to match my ego. I slowly thumbed those rolls out of the fabric, elastic film pouches in the lid of my lens bag for clerk while describing, bashfully, modestly the horrendous conditions under which I had to carry out my art. I dropped a few names, using them as casually as someone who had known them for years. I let that clerk know how lucky he was that I chose him to take care of my film. I asked for more than service, I asked him to hold my trust.

When I returned to pick up the images which I had had thumb nailed onto a few slices of the choicest of photographic papers, as I slouched with the burden of my greatness on the counter, the clerk returned with a slight smirk on his face. He lay the contact sheets before me, one at a time. And, behold, all of them were blank. "Did you synch your flash with your F2?" I looked at the smirking clerk, with what I hoped amounted to a look of condescension. It was not to be. "Do you have the developed rolls?" He pulled them out from behind his back. They were browny-orange and blank.

Helen Keller once said that "Life is either a daring adventure or nothing." Life is that big, red button. I stand under the door, with my finger playing on it. I'd bet it's been disconnected. No way of knowing, however, until I push it. There are no instructions, no clear sense of what one ought to do with it, just the threat of a penalty if things go wrong. As one who has pushed that button and experienced the consequences, I can tell you assuredly that there is no better way to get a sense of what the button is for than to push it, and see what happens. There is sometimes a penalty to be paid, but none quite so high as the penalty incurred by refusing to push it.

Originally published in the Globe and Mail, Facts & Arguments,
August 23, 2006.

18

VIOLIN MALADY

HUDDLED IN THE WAITING room, my daughter coughs, and sits playing with a stuffed toy frog, chatting with it as she prepares herself for her appointment. Last week, they worked on her elbow, and she's still having trouble with it. They're still working on a problem she has with her hand. Weekly operations and visits to a specialist.

She sighs first, then smiles to the frog, knowing that she will get through it somehow. Some weeks are better than others, but she knows some of this week's news is going to be bad, because it is every week. She lives with a condition that can never be properly healed. This is what ails her: the violin.

Her diagnosis, one that shall plague her for the next few years at least, perhaps the rest of her life, is this: she does not know how to play it. This is a malady that her music teacher has pointed out, and one that she continues to diagnose in its subtle stages as Elise takes her medicine.

Each week we visit Susan, the physic who attends to her condition. She diagnoses the biggest two or three current problems, and writes out her prescriptions. Elise is told, gently, how horrible her condition is, and given a weekly remedy, which she must carry out.

My daughter suffers from an ailing ignorance. Ignorance is a common condition. It's natural and when left alone, comfortable—a state of ease. But, she discovered that she was ignorant of something she considered critical to her survival. First, a curiosity infected her unknowing. The curiosity degraded with a fever into desire. A desire to know poisoned her ignorance, tumoured her thoughts, and became dis-eased. A malignant ignorance. This disease cried for cure.

Elise initially chose the violin because it began with the letter 'v'. It seemed exotic. But, like many sicknesses, it germed her insides, without invitation or clear cause, and worked its way out. Her fingers found notes, her bow stroked notes into the air. In an odd way, though she knew no one who played this instrument, she could explain it, somehow, and it could explain her. She learned to pull the black lumps from the music staff and make her violin speak them. And all this, rather than inoculating her, deepened her need to know. The violin grew on her.

The door to the Purple Room opens (each room in the music studio is a different colour) and Susan steps out smiling but tired, releasing her latest patient. My daughter stands, places the frog on her chair and slowly steps forward. Into the Purple room she goes. Susan smiles at me and closes the door behind her.

I wait in a soft chair, partly reading a book, but partly listening for the sounds of her therapy. I hear parallel cries of two violins working through the beginnings of "Minuet

3." I hear them repeat a section. It's the fingering, I guess, as the note from one violin slides down to join the other pitch. That's all I need to hear. I need the sense that she's getting better, some how, in some way. Notes of Elise's lesson blend with a student stumbling up a scale on the piano, and someone carefully singing Birch Canoe off key. The teacher repeatedly bangs a note on the piano inviting the student to reach its pitch. All sick. All struggling. This studio is a ward for the musically ill.

Sometimes her violin causes convulsions. There's often talk of quitting, for the wooden tumour on her neck annoys her, frustrates her, attacks her sense of herself, growing fibrous roots into her inoperable being. But then, after her strong words, something violent and tender overcomes her and she doctors Joe (her name for her violin) like he's a teddy bear.

The Purple Room's door opens and Susan steps out, her smile haggard. The patient walks out, stooped with the responsibility of the remedy. The prognosis has improved, and, this round of treatment, by the looks of it, is partially successful. "She needs to work on her bow this week. Don't let her move her elbow. That way her bowing will improve. It'll help her move her hand properly too." She turns toward Elise. "Make sure you read the bow marks on Minuet 3, OK?" My daughter nods and grins. The diagnosis and she's happy. Happy and sick. So much more to go before her music teacher will ever declare her terminally well. "See you next week," Susan adds.

"See you next week," Elise repeats. She sets her jaw and smiles; we will treat her condition for another week. There's so much more to go: the road to complete recovery, lifelong.

Yet, the violin is one of her favourite diseases. She nurses the infection, and dotes on it, because without it she will never be well.

Originally published as "The violin, bow and some music" in the Globe and Mail, Facts & Arguments, January 18, 2007.

19

THE NEW STUDENT

COSMIC MASSES OF INFORMATION are changing our students. The vast quantities of information students experience transform them into a new species of learner. The amount of information they encounter is unprecedented and alters the complexion of education.

Information is proliferating at a rate that would make a rabbit blush. A University of California at Berkley study estimates the total volume of information generated annually as being 2 exabytes (2 X 1018) of unique information every year—250 megabytes for every person on earth.

Students are exposed to vast amounts of information in their leisure time. A 2001 Media Awareness Network study reports that after school, 9- to 17-year-old Canadians like to listen to music, watch TV, visit with friends, and surf the Internet. Television, the Internet, and music expose them to more information than ever before.

Teens watch TV 12.9 hours a week. In 1952, there were only 146,000 televisions in Canada, and only a single channel. By 1972, 97 per cent of Canadian homes had at least one

TV. Statistics Canada reports that by 2005, Eighty-eight per cent of the country received at least 36 channels.

Massive amounts of information flow through the TV.

The Internet is a close second behind TV. A 2005 Media Awareness Network study reports that 94 per cent of youth report Internet access from home. Ipsos Reid revealed that users spent an average of 12.7 hours a week online in 2005. Cyveillance estimates that the Internet contains 2.1 billion pages, and grows by 7 million pages a day. Five hundred million screens of information, says the Pennsylvania Department of Education, travel the Internet weekly "making more information available...than at any other period in the history of the world." The student's biggest exposure to information comes through the Internet.

Canadian students carry vast amounts of music in their pockets. Smaller MP3 players store around 240 songs. If the average vinyl album holds an approximate average of 12 songs per release, smaller MP3s hold around 120 albums worth of information. Big MP3s can hold 25,000 songs— the equivalent of 2083 LPs.

TV, Internet, music. All three expose the new student to a mammoth universe of information.

This exposure is not leaving youth unscathed. There are at least seven educational trends that can be traced to the new student adapting to large quantities of information.

The first trend is a negative impact on reading. A growing group of people, for instance, know how to read, but choose not to, a phenomenon termed "aliteracy." The National Endowment for the Arts discovered that the reading of literature dropped 28 per cent for young adults between 1982 and 2002. Like most people, students read because they must, which means most choose not to read in their spare time. The way we read is changing too. Linton Weeks noted in the Washington Post that readers increasingly skim texts and don't really read in a traditional sense at all. People scan text without fully understanding it.

The second trend is information recycling. In a world littered with information, information reuse seems almost natural. Information is "re-purposed" from its original context and redeployed.

It's a huge trend in information management circles. The new student discovered a similar value. Librarian Joyce Roby says "We are faced with the `cut and paste' generation who go online and cut and paste from various articles, piecing the bits together to call their own." Of course, plagiarism is one form of the cut and paste trend. Is it any wonder that it's escalating?

The third trend is the growing importance of the search. As one might expect, the new student is not interested in how to originate information, but, rather, how to find it. Author Paul Horowitz claims that "students need to learn how to Google." He adds that "Google is making such `librarian skills' obsolete while simultaneously raising concerns about what new knowledge students will need if they are to manage their new-found powers wisely."

The fourth trend is the decline of the book and library. A 2001 Pew Internet & American Life Project survey reports 71 per cent of teens online rely mostly on Internet sources for research. 24 per cent relied mostly on the library. The two main reasons students preferred Internet research were speed and the ease of use. The Nova Scotia Department of Education reports that "in 1990, there were

103 teacher-librarians in Nova Scotia; in 2002, there were 9." The Internet has hit books and libraries hard.

The fifth trend is the emphasis on speed. Speed is a part of the information volume itself and is addictive. Matt Richtel, in The New York Times, reports that high information volumes can produce symptoms similar to Attention Deficit Disorder. Those affected tend to become "frustrated with long-term projects, thrive on the stress of constant fixes of information."

Information produces a dopamine-induced, narcotic-like high that uses the same "pathway as our drugs of abuse and pleasure." A Reuters study reported that the "PC generation is the generation of information addiction. Almost half of respondents said if data was a drug, they knew addicts, and the Internet is pinpointed as a key driver." The classroom is quiet when compared to the Internet. It isn't surprising, then, that students are often bored in the classroom. A study done on Indiana high school students revealed that two out of three students report being bored in class every day.

The sixth trend is weakening thinking skills. A CREPUQ-sponsored survey conducted in 2003 shows that Québec university students experience major difficulties conducting research as many "have limited knowledge, or no knowledge, of basic elements characterizing the information research process." Laura Sessions Stepp, in the Washington Post, reports that students "value information-gathering over deliberation, breadth over depth, and other people's arguments over their own." The new student can cut and paste, but is having trouble thinking.

Parker Palmer calls thinking a process that allows "one idea to generate another in us." The resistance to thought comes from at least two sources. First, thinking produces more information.

Second, thought requires time and sustained effort, an extravagance in a speed-oriented world.

The seventh trend is a growing tolerance of error. Students simply don't have the time to assess each bit of information with any thought whatsoever. If one "Googles" Pierre Trudeau, he or she is returned 396,000 hits. "Stephen Harper, Prime Minister" brings 1,170,000 hits. "Riel Rebellion" brings a modest 43,000 hits. The new student learns to make snap judgments usually based on intuition. "Close" now counts in horseshoes, hand-grenades, atom bombs and knowledge.

Parker Palmer defines a good education as one that "teaches students to become both producers of knowledge and discerning consumers of what other people claim to know." But these seven trends suggest that the new student is a species more resistant to traditional educational endeavours than ever before. Though the new student represents what our world is coming to, the traditional education has never been more important.

As the gap between the new student and the traditional teacher grows, the new education must find ways to bridge the two.

Originally published in the Globe and Mail, June 26, 2007.

20

MAKING A BEELINE FOR THE EXIT

Not long ago, I found the body of a bee: its wings carefully tucked together; its body curled into a ball; its legs folded together the way, perhaps, a lawn chair is folded to be put away.

The black-and-yellow bristles were clean and combed; the wings like panels of plain stained glass folded back and glowing.

Its body faced east, toward the morning sun. Not the work of a mortician. Although this bee died alone and far from its home, this was a thoughtful exit by a creature who took time to put itself away when it was finished.

I took the bee home where I could study it in more detail because I loved the kind of death it suggested.

As I study its body, I realize death did not surprise it. It knew death was coming, and instead of fighting it, gave in, stopped and pulled itself together before leaving. I suppose the other possibility is that the bee has some control over when it releases its life spark.

Either way, this bee reveals a gift that exceeds what is given to most humans.

I can remember the first time I found the body of a dead dragonfly. I was walking down the sidewalk when I came upon the burnished blue body parked in the middle of the walk. I thought it was resting, facing the sun, wings outstretched, so I watched for a few minutes.

I slowly realized that it was oddly still. I finally worked up the nerve to touch the abdomen, and when I did the body toppled over. It had been dead for some time.

One recent morning, I found another dragonfly I thought had died. It was grasping the top of a blade of grass, facing the sunrise. I judged it dead because its wings were white and frozen with the first frost of the season. And that is how they tend to go: They land, wings spread as though they may burst into flight again at any time. But if one pokes and prods the body of this creature, one finds it dead. Like a plane left on an airstrip: the pilot has left his machine and gone home.

This smaller dragonfly hadn't quit this world yet. It turns out it was waiting, waiting for its wings to thaw and dry, to see if it would fly another day. Nevertheless, I know this to be true of dragonflies: They often die well.

Insects do not die well indoors. A quick check of a windowsill after a summer day can confirm this. The common housefly can be found lying on its back, at odd angles, wings askew, as though some kind of struggle has occurred, as though the insect has been assaulted and killed.

They have struggled, of course, with the glass of the window. The light coming through the window seems to call them and the glass holds them back, which whips the critter into a final frenzy.

That struggle continues until the insect falls lifeless to the windowsill, the contortions and position of the carcass evidence of the terror and struggle that took them to death.

The noble dragonfly and bee will die poorly behind glass as well. They, too, are drawn to the light like many insects, but the glass destroys their repose and they die kicking and deformed.

Once the dragonfly I found had thawed out, it startled me by throwing itself against the window in my office. I watched it do headstands and lie on its back as it attempted to bore through the glass.

If I had left it there, it would have died in ignominy. The same is true of the bumblebee. Bumblebees only bumble on the inside of a window.

Scientifically speaking, the light is said to orient these creatures. But it does more than merely orient them—the light calls them forward. If the creature cannot move forward, toward the light (or perhaps, if it senses a diminished light) it seems to panic, throw temper tantrums and careen wildly to its end.

Insects must be drawn to the light, and as long as they can head toward it unimpeded they're calm, and they die well. When they are prevented from moving toward that light, they seem frantic and die panicked and deprived. Am I less of a creature for being content behind this glass?

These creatures, in this sense, are worshippers of light. There seems to be nothing more intolerable to them than to be separated from their god.

It's as though an insect needs to know that there is nothing between it and the light in order to be comfortable. If it is comfortable then everything is fine, even death.

All the insects I have found who have died well die facing the light. Their position suggests that when they die, all will be well if the long journey to the sun can be made directly.

If it is not too much to ask, I would like to die like this bee, facing the sun and composed. Let me die like a dragonfly: wings poised, outstretched, legs lighted on a sidewalk, like the first half of a mighty jump out of time and into eternity.

Originally published in the Globe and Mail, Facts & Arguments,
October 25, 2007.

21

DO WE SUFFER FROM TECHNOLOGICAL AUTISM?

I'M MID-WAY INTO A conversation with a man when he quickly raises his hand to his ear. "I've got to take this," he says, and turns away from me. After waiting for half a minute, I walk away.

"Your son just scored," I tell another man who's thumbing his BlackBerry as he sits with his daughter at a soccer game. He grunts and looks up, foggy at first, but gradually his mind takes its place in the stands with the rest of us.

At the table next to me, yet a third man chatted on the telephone while ordering his food, gesticulating and pointing. He jimmies and jerks his way through a lunch order, clearly not listening to the caller nor the waitress.

After these incidents, I joked to a group of people that technology causes autism. But as I said it, I made a mental note to check on the official diagnosis of autism and make the comparison.

Autism, in sum, is a significantly reduced sensitivity to context. Though no one has termed it autism, pervasive users of technology are often said to be suffering from other

Hymns of Home

ailments: iPod oblivion, cellphone zombieism, inattention blindness, problem cellphone use, or the CrackBerry prayer (named after the pose one strikes while discreetly checking his or her device).

How much sensitivity is lost under the influence of technology? Jim Balsillie, CEO of BlackBerry maker Research in Motion, suggests BlackBerry use means a person is 20 per cent "not there." However, An investigator who published a driving and cellphone study in The New England Journal of Medicine reported "a 50-per-cent reduction in the processing of visual information." So a person engaged in the use of technology is, according to some experts, at least 50 per cent "not there."

Translate that into real life and you see the problem. Senator Liz Krueger of New York is currently seeking to ban pedestrian use of portable electronics because of "iPod oblivion." In January, a 23-year-old man reportedly absorbed in his iPod was struck as he stepped off of a curb. A few months earlier another man stepped in front of a city bus. Fifty per cent "not there" often leads to 100 per cent "not there."

According to the American Psychological Association's Diagnostic and Statistical Manual of Mental Disorders, Fourth Edition (DSM: IV), the diagnostic criteria for the autistic disorder requires the confirmation of three major features:

1. A qualitative impairment in social interaction.

2. A qualitative impairment in communication.

3. Restricted repetitive and stereotyped patterns of behaviour, interests and activities.

The first feature to confirm is the "qualitative impairment in social interaction." The confirmation requires that we observe a "marked impairment in the use of multiple non-verbal behaviours such as eye-to-eye gaze, facial expression, body posture, and gestures to regulate social interaction."

A friend shared with me a scene he recently saw that summed up the BlackBerry and family perfectly. In the front of a Lexus SUV sat a dad, deep in BlackBerry prayer, his young son, sat in the back seat of this vehicle, sulking and silent. "It's a moment that perfectly captures our times," he declared.

Numbers of children have hidden, flushed, or destroyed cellphones or PDAs to rid themselves of unwanted competition. In an article for the Wall Street Journal, Katherine Rosman interviews nine-year-old Bob Ledbetter, who reports fighting with his father to get him to put down his BlackBerry. Bob is unable to get his attention. "Sometimes I think he's deaf," he says.

Not only does technology help cause these symptoms, but it trains users into autistic-like behaviours. Blogger Charles Green wrote about a recent experience getting his hearing check in mid October: The audiologist related she'd noticed a lot of people in their 40s had started coming in with concerns about their hearing, but their tests usually came back just fine. As Green relates, his doctor blames cellphones and handheld computing devices. "These people have lost the ability to pay attention for more than a few seconds," Green quotes his audiologist as saying. "When the conversation requires more attention, they zone out, and lose connection."

Three other observations can confirm the "qualitative impairment in social interaction" are the "failure to develop peer relationships appropriate to the developmental level"; a "lack of spontaneous seeking to share enjoyment, interest, or achievements with other people"; and "a lack of emotional reciprocity."

The Journal's Rosman reports in her interview with Emma Colonna, a 9th-grader who repeatedly catches her parents texting during family outings: In the middle of Emma's eighth-grade awards ceremony, at dinner, and in darkened movie theatres. "During my dance recital," she says, "I'm 99% sure they were emailing except while I was on stage."

The DSM:IV lists a second diagnostic feature: "qualitative impairment of communication." One of four observations is needed to confirm this feature. I think it would be easiest to observe "in individuals with adequate speech" a "marked impairment in the ability to initiate or sustain a conversation with others."

In fact, a "qualitative impairments of communication" is part of the point for some users. The Carphone Warehouse commissioned a survey of 16,500 people and discovered that 42 per cent believe it is reasonable to use a text message to avoid conversation, if it is done politely. The same study found that 21 per cent of the study group used their cellphones to prevent people from approaching them. There are numerous complaints from spouses and children that devices like BlackBerrys impair familial communication. Many companies have banned them in meetings for the same reason.

Reporter Dan Harris interviewed the General Manager of Sheraton Chicago, who admitted he wrote emails at the supper table while his wife tried to engage him in conversation. Harris interviewed Gayle Porter from Rutgers

University School of Business. She said that some users are prepared to give up family time or time with friends to attend to these gadgets. In extreme situations, people, she says, "will give up taking care of themselves." Sometimes the impairment is deliberate. Sometimes the impairment is not.

The final feature according to the DSM: IV is this: Do technology users have "restricted repetitive and stereotyped patterns of behaviour, interests and activities?" Of the four observations that confirm this feature, I think this one is easiest: "apparently inflexible adherence to specific, non-functional routines or rituals."

In her article for the Washington Post, Kathrine Rosman notes one family forbids their mother from using her mobile device from suppertime until the children's bedtime. The mother hid her device in the bathroom and visited the powder room frequently to stay in touch. According to this mother, "the kids think I have a small bladder."

Checking the device is its own little ritual cum obsession. Many users have reported hearing the cellphone ring or feeling it vibrate, but when they check it, no one is there. This phenomenon has been dubbed "ringxiety." A survey done by David Laramie for his dissertation noted that two-thirds of all adults have experienced "ringxiety." He found that the often people use their phones, the more likely they are to experience ringxiety.

Do technology users exhibit qualitative impairments in social interaction and communication? Yes and yes. Do they demonstrate "restrictive repetitive and stereotyped patterns of behaviour." Yes.

Diagnosis: technological autism.

Definition: A pervasive disorder induced through the use of technology.

Originally published in the Globe and Mail, October 22, 2007.

22

AWAY FROM THE MANGER

O NE CHRISTMAS, LINDA BOUGHT the kids a plastic manger scene. She bought it because she wanted the children to interact with the figures, play with the players, major and minor. It's a hands-on type of thing, she argued. I agreed with her. There's no better way to get into a story than being able to interact with it in some physical way. All the season's big stars—The baby Christ, the angels, shepherds, Joseph, Mary, and the barnyard cast— built from durable, kid-friendly plastic.

At the beginning of December, when we decorated the house for Christmas, we set up the new manger scene. However, we had forgotten about the democracy of toys. In this republic, all toys, regardless of symbolic value, are created equal. And, any toys may interact, depending on the elasticity of the operator's imagination. Understandably, Christ and cast were popular. Everyone seemed to want him around. Hence, there was a desire to mix them with every other toy. Christ simply would not stay put.

The baby Jesus ended up visiting with our Lego populants often. He frequented the company of stuffed animals, despite the immense difference in scale. Another time, I found Jesus stuffed into the chimney of a dollhouse. He was helping his brother, Santa, the kids explained. I found him driving the Barbie Corvette with Barbie, down at the end of the hall. The rest of the cast took their cue from the baby. I saw a wiseman and the donkey, helping a farmer drive a tractor in a castle. I found Mary and another wiseman helping a set of Lego firemen rescue animals and plastic, medieval soldiers from a wooden train wreck. It was as if the manger was only a pose, like a picture taken at a party that the manger cast would strike for a moment, a starting point from which they would begin.

Then, Jesus lost his head. One of our children or one of their friends broke the head off the plastic Jesus. I mean, he was a toy, and the heads of toys are often removable. A child tried removing his head but ended up breaking it off. The creator of the toy obviously felt that Jesus' head should not come off.

In our hearts, we were deeply disturbed. It was OK for Barbie to lose her head, or Ken to lose his, but not the Christ-child. Who would do such a thing? Why not one of the shepherds. Why not Joseph? But the body was found headless, the plastic neck snapped in two. We searched for the head—in the big Lego tub. In the toy boxes in people's rooms. In drawers and under beds. No head.

Who had beheaded the Christ-child? This was a deliberate act. I had stepped on Jesus on another day but he hadn't lost his head. Someone had obviously wanted to pull his head off. So began our crusade. "Who took Jesus' head?" We asked, and we heard silence. We asked the question several different ways: we asked calmly, urgently, quietly, sadly, happily, indifferently, and with deep concern. Nothing. Or, rather, everything. Elise thought she saw it in various places throughout the house (that made us suspect her). May insisted she hadn't done anything (which made us suspect her). Ezra got tired of us asking the question and confessed (which made us conclude it was him) but then his story wouldn't hold (which made us suspect him). Each one carried shades of an unsinkable guilt. Linda and I, too, once we embarked on the inquisition, felt pangs of guilt. Maybe they hadn't broken it. Maybe they were all telling the truth. The inquisition ended in failure.

We phoned the manufacturer and asked them to ship a new Jesus. They could make no guarantees, but we hoped that his arrival might happen before Christmas Day. In the meantime, the headless Jesus was too much to look at, to take at this season, so to soften his look my wife crazy-glued the head of a Lego person on his shoulders. The sunglassed eyes of the Lego head looked far too smug to sit on Christ's shoulders, and the head also would accept a number of different hats or helmets, all which seemed simply blasphemous, but it was much better than a headless baby.

Many years earlier, Linda and I had traveled to Rome, to the Sistine Chapel, to see Michelangelo's frescos. I remember staring up at the roof, considering, with the rest of the ruck, the space between God and Adam. What could the space mean? What was Michelangelo's thought? The space in Michelangelo's painting I think was a practical consideration. If the two hands had touched, things would have gotten weird.

The new Jesus arrived in a small box a few days before Christmas. Was this the advent or the second coming? He was more popular than ever. Despite our sternest warnings he consorted regularly with all toys, regardless of their shape and size, regardless of where they were made. He, obviously, wasn't going to stay in the manger, though the picture on the manger scene box suggested this might happen.

It's time to set up our manger scene again. I arrange the figurines on the coffee table, according to the picture on the box. As I lay Christ into his molded plastic manger, I realize, he won't be here long. Within minutes, the last place I'll find him is in the manger. For in our house, God can be touched, so there's no telling where he might end up.

Originally published in the Globe and Mail, Facts & Arguments, December 17, 2007.

2 3

IN PRAISE OF WALKING]

A COUPLE MONTHS AGO, I was crossing a quiet street in a crosswalk to go to a park. I had with me five children. A driver, seeing a small gap between me and three of the children, decided to dart between the two groups of pedestrians in the crosswalk. Last week, crossing in a crosswalk, a Black Dodge pickup truck passed an arm's-length in front of me.

I walk to and from work, and I walk for fun, which puts me on the streets of Calgary more than 300 times a year for 20 minutes or more each outing, for the last 12 years. I will confess to you, that I don't always cross at crosswalks. I'm also an avid jaywalker.

I jaywalk because I believe it is safer. I cross 22 streets on my way to and from work each day. Six of the crossings I use are busy streets. I cross at a crosswalk six or seven times each day, and jaywalk the rest. Most days, my pedestrian rights are flattened in a crosswalk at least once a day.

This morning, during a light snow, a brazen woman in a black Lexus SUV saw me in the crosswalk and drove on through. I have never been threatened in the same way by any driver when I jaywalk. It's simply never happened.

In 2006, Calgary drivers hit 538 pedestrians. In 190 cases, the drivers were charged. Pedestrians were charged in 25 situations. By the end of October of 2007, 428 pedestrians kissed some chrome. The pedestrian was charged 25 times, and the driver 146. Walking within the paint isn't as safe as it seems.

Why are crosswalks so dangerous? They're dangerous because one of every 20 drivers does not respect the pedestrian's right to cross the street. They're dangerous because pedestrians expect drivers to respect those rights, even when drivers aren't paying attention. For me, a defensive posture requires me to expect disrespectful drivers, to expect drivers to drive toward me deliberately (which has happened on occasion), to believe all traffic is out to get me—in short, adopt a healthy paranoia.

I am paranoid when I jaywalk. Since I'm crossing without any rights as a pedestrian, I'm alert; I expect traffic to be mean-spirited and vicious. I cross in such a way as to minimize my intrusion to traffic streams, and to protect myself as much as possible. When I use a crosswalk, I take less responsibility for my passage. I rely, I would suggest, too heavily on the power of white paint and the good will and attention of others.

Two weeks ago, a mother pushing her child in a stroller entered a crosswalk. Halfway through her crossing, a man driving a city truck, talking on his cellphone, flew through the crosswalk and, noticing the terrified mother and child mere feet from the front of his pickup, managed to let go of the steering wheel to give a wave with his impish grin, as if to say in a jaunty way "Sorry about nearly killing you and your child."

There is a $500 fine for driving through a crosswalk with a pedestrian in it. This is a good thing. The only issue I have with this fine is that it is most often awarded posthumously, as a bequest of the pedestrian.

When I taught my own children to cross the street, I tried to teach them of the power of the crosswalk. However, I realize if I want my children to learn to cross the street safely, I should teach them to jaywalk—that they should take complete responsibility for crossing the street. Don't leave it to mothers who organize soccer teams on cellphones while they drive, or men who eat hamburgers while they steer with their knees.

On the street, it's only a lump of humanity against a screaming metal machine. In this duel, one must leave aside intangibles like courtesy and the law and realize that the motored metal always outdoes the loping lump.

I recommend we eliminate all crosswalks and all pedestrian rights as assigned by the laws of our city and province. Instead, Calgary should announce open season on pedestrians with no hunting limit. We could offer stuffing and mounting services for anyone who manages to bag a pedestrian crossing a street. The only ones hit would be the weak and unaware—thus improving the species. In this new regime, pedestrians would clearly understand what they need to do to safely cross the street.

Originally published in Fast Forward Magazine, March 20, 2008.

24

THE CUP MAKES THE COFFEE

I t's Melmac. My latest coffee cup.

It's a beauty from the 1960s. I stole it from the summer camp I volunteer with.

A flesh-coloured, sculpted treasure, it's been filled about six times this morning already.

I just went to the office coffee pot, filled it, got into a short conversation on the way back, drained it in the three minutes of talk, then returned to the coffee pot, filled it again and returned to my office.

I'm working hard at drinking coffee, the way it suggests I should. Sip. Sip. Sip. It holds very little, and the coffee stays hot all the way to the bottom.

It is small because it is a cup that is meant to be around a group of people, all of whom are sharing a pot of coffee. It takes a part of the pot but leaves plenty for others. Little polite sips with lots of talk in between, a value also promoted by the teacup.

However, my Melmac cup is meant to be more animated than a teacup, which is designed to sit primly on its saucer.

It is a cup that can be waved in the air while one talks, since it is worn like a ring on the index finger.

Coffee is the happy addition to friendship. My Melmac special is designed to be used in the direct vicinity of a coffee pot. It emphasizes the delight one feels from pouring yet another cup.

This is not a cup to walk with, as I have learned many times. The brown spots on my clothing and shoes attest to this learning.

I set it down next to the mother ship of coffee cups—my sailing mug. It's a greedy, navy-blue tank that holds more than half a pot of coffee below deck.

A mat of soft rubber covers the bottom. Its wide, cone shape lowers the mug's centre of gravity, decreasing the odds of tipping it. The shape also encourages spurts of coffee, splashing up because of turbulence, to fall back into the cup rather than outside of it.

It has a lid with a spout for coffee flow that can be opened like the valve of a fire hydrant, one that fits into my mouth and is designed to reduce spills. The lid is not a device that encourages economical sipping, but big, smutty, open-throated drafts after which I wipe my face clean with my sleeve.

The mug treats coffee more like a fuel than an accoutrement, to be drunk in situations when conversation is not necessary, perhaps when one is alone. Coffee quality is clearly less important than quantity.

The bottom is meant to grip unsteady, flat surfaces. This is a cup meant to stabilize a large amount of coffee for a long haul. It does not like cars, nor is it meant for driving. It takes two hands to manage it—one hand to hold it, one to open and close the lid.

But my copper-coloured mug with a chrome-rimmed lid, it loves the car. It's built for the cup holder. The lid has a valve on it that can be opened with the same hand that holds the handle.

Like my sailing mug, this cup promotes drinking coffee while doing something else. In this sense, it suggests whatever coffee it carries is not worthy of one's full attention.

In many cases, my cup is right: The coffee does not deserve special attention. So drink while you drive. Or drink while you meet. It suggests coffee is likely to be imported a fair distance, the pot nowhere close. It also cares about my clothes more than most mugs: It wants me to look good. An elaborate array of rubber rings locks the liquid within.

At home, I have two French bowls meant for drinking coffee. They're white, wide-mouthed dishes I could use for breakfast cereal if I wanted to. They hold a great deal of coffee, but the bowl requires two hands, and one cannot move while drinking.

The wide mouth insists that the coffee be sipped. Drinking too fast means I wear most of the beverage.

The bowl insists that the drinker sit calmly, and that he or she sit for a while. The drinker will not be getting up and down or talking and gesticulating energetically. The drinker is not to be driving, dressing or in a meeting. The drinker is made to sit and confront the brew.

With that much attention on the coffee, it had better be good.

Cup choice is at least as important as the coffee itself. It's not so much a container as a philosophy of coffee, answering the big beverage questions: what coffee's good for, how it should be enjoyed and how life should be lived around it.

The cup amounts to at least half of what I expect when I take a sip.

Originally published in the Globe and Mail, Facts & Arguments, April 2, 2008.

25

GOODBYE TO THE LAKE

WE TOOK A CHANCE, our first year, and booked a little motel on the lakeshore. It was perfect. My son rose at 6, even on holiday. I made a pot of coffee while he ate breakfast. Then we walked a few steps from the door of our motel room to the beach.

After a quick survey of the sand, we would choose a spot for the chairs and beach umbrella. He would chase ducks, build sandcastles, investigate the lake bottom in the clear, still morning water. Set up on the beach's best real estate, we would wait for the world to wake up. I would read for a while, sip coffee, study the water, consult on sandcastle design, engage in construction.

Then as others slowly filled the beach, a sea of children took control of their kid world of sand, candy, inflatable plastic and water. It was the kind of holiday I remember. It was the kind of holiday I wanted to give my three kids. And it had to involve water.

The swimming area had a dock anchored a few metres offshore. The lake had minnows and frogs. And it was hot. In the heat of the afternoon, we would rent a boat from an old lady and ride out to the middle of the lake for a swim.

We were there for a couple of years, and then someone came in and ripped the motel off its foundations and began to prepare the ground for condos. No problem, we thought. We'll just go to the campground next door and stay in one of their cabins.

Summer, 2004. The feel of our new destination was different but similar. A little cabin in a family campground in a park designed and built by the owner of nearly 35 years.

There was a tepee in the middle. At 7 each night there were videos in the tepee for the kids. A homemade mini-golf course was lined with jig-sawed, painted cartoon characters. Handcrafted by a man who loved his land. The candy store carried items for a single penny.

In the late morning a local baker would drive into the campground with fresh-baked goods in a beat-up station wagon, a speaker mounted on top, blaring the daily specials. The owner of the campground had a car with a speaker stuck on the roof, too, and he would roll slowly through the tents and cabins announcing an activity or the daily plans he'd made.

On his property, kids ran free in hordes. They roved from site to site, collecting bottles and cans to return at the candy store. Early in the evening, the owner would light a beach fire and supply marshmallows and sticks. One night a week was fireworks night and most of the tenants would buy a stick or two and contribute them to a show launched from the beach.

We tried to book a cabin there the following year, but couldn't. The owner had sold his property to a developer. They were putting in condos.

So we moved to a little lakeside motel up the lake. It too

had a lovely culture, with a trampoline, a candy store, water and sand. And some time while we were staying at this little rundown motel, it sold. The trampoline, we were informed by the developer, would be shut down soon because of liability issues. The old lady we rented boats from had to move off the beach and was looking to sell her boats. Beachfront was too expensive, she said.

Construction crews ranged up and down the roads. Real estate agents picketed property. Massive concrete footings were dug into the sand. Sounds of saws and straining engines wafted over the water.

One of our last nights, we ate supper on the roof of the pizza-gelato-photofinishing-fireworks-video rental-drugstore and went to D Dutchman Dairy for ice cream cones. On the way home I decided to tour our old campground (bad idea).

The gates had been knocked down to allow construction vehicles free access. I drove in. The grounds had been razed. Trees cut down. Tent sites bulldozed. Candy store windows smashed. Along the mini-golf course, the remaining cartoon figures scrutinized a man who seemed to be intoxicated staggering toward them. He set his drink down so he could swing his sledgehammer with both hands. While we watched, he knocked a hole in the candy store wall.

The children leapt into rage, which crested and fell into guttural sorrow. He wasn't bashing a building: He was hammering our holiday. Like a funeral for a friend where someone assaults the corpse.

In four years, the lake utterly transformed. The kitschy motels and campground disappeared, replaced with gated communities and concierges. The old holiday at the lake was grubby, loud and social. The new is clean, quiet and insulated. The old culture let my family live on the lake for $100 a night. I can buy my piece of the new, beginning, as the advertisement declares, in the low 400s.

Originally published in the Globe and Mail, Facts & Arguments,
July 14, 2008.

26

TAKE A WALK

THERE IS ONLY ONE way humans are made to move. They are made to walk. There are many other ways to get around. You can canoe, for instance. Or paraglide. Or jog. But these modes of transportation are not the staple of human mobility. Walking is unavoidable, a necessity for those with two working legs.

The entire scheme of nature, and the human's place within it, is built around the understanding that humans use their legs to move. It's a great unspoken assumption. The earth expects humans to walk.

Wildlife expects humans to walk, and it has trouble with other forms of transport. North American drivers kill 1 million animals each day, nearly 12 animals per second. Four hundred million animals are killed by drivers in North America each year. Almost 2 million deer are killed on North American roads yearly.

According to the National Institute for Urban Wildlife and U.S. Fish and Wildlife Service, 50 to 100 million birds are killed each year by vehicles. Research reports that road-kill is a significant factor in the decline of amphibians.

Motorized transport dramatically reduces insect populations.

Though humans invented vehicles, we have trouble understanding them, too. The 210 million vehicles on North America's 4.5 million miles of roads cause 47,000 human deaths a year. But, how many mammals, birds, amphibians and humans would be hurt or killed if humans only walked?

A walker is not likely to "run over" a gopher when she walks. If she waded into a stream, she's unlikely to step on a fish. All creatures, in this sense, understand walking. Walking is a primal transport, expected by the world's animals and the land itself, evidence of an ancient arrangement between humans and their world.

Walking serves as a bridge between other humans and other animals. Humans tend to walk between 2 and 5 miles per hour—an average of around 3 miles per hour. Dogs walk at speeds between 2 and 4 miles per hour. Camels walk an average speed of 3 miles per hour. Horses and mules, when walking, operate at speeds of 3 to 4 miles per hour. Elephant walk at 4 miles per hour. The old friendships between humans and some animals partly depend on a shared walking speed. A walking pace is the speed of community.

Though we don't walk with many other animals, we could. Many other animals share a similar pace: bears, mice, ants, snakes, cats, aardvarks. The ordinary human can keep pace with a puma, a zebra, a rhinoceros or an American president.

Yet, humans are obsessed with the top speeds of each living thing. Many sources announce, for example, that the elk has a top speed of 25 mph. Very few note the walking speed: between 3 and 5 mph.

As part of that obsession, humans find ways to travel faster every year. Usain Bolt's recent Olympic sprint averaged 23 mph. When he sprints, he is unique, and alone. When he walks, any walking human can keep pace. Top speed emphasizes difference.

Mechanically assisted types of transport alienate humans from their planet, and from one another. The fastest humans, currently, ride in the space shuttle traveling at 18,685 mph in orbit; 18,685 mph is an unearthly speed. Top speeds separate us from one another and alienate us from the earth. Lower speeds unify us and bind us to our planet.

For those who like speed, there is a price to pay. One cost is tension. When you drive, the mind is consumed, for the most part, in the exercise of managing extra speed, paying attention, watching for potholes and pedestrians. Even jogging requires more attention than walking.

Researchers report that the faster you travel the more tension you experience. A number of studies observe, for example, that when speed increases, negative emotions intensify. This factor alone plays a large role in what has been termed "road rage."

Another cost is a diminished sense of context. When you walk, your field of vision is nearly 180 degrees, 140 degrees of which feeds your awareness. The Optometrists Association of Australia reports that human field of vision "is reduced with increasing speed." For example, at 62 mph, field of vision contracts to 40 degrees.

Higher speeds cause peripheral vision to "smudge," which hampers object recognition, and lowers response times. Motorists traveling 25 mph or faster have more difficulty determining whether a pedestrian is ready to cross a street, and in consequence have more difficulty deciding whether they should slow down.

In other words, speed impedes thinking and decision-making. Thought depends on perception, but speed impairs it. Things "come out of nowhere." Collisions become inevitable. So walk.

Begin. Choose a walk of a reasonable length. Start with once a week. A 5-minute drive from your home, at average city speeds, amounts to a 25-minute walk, one way. Select a quiet route, as thought speaks with a quiet voice. You should be able to hear the sound of your own steps as you walk. Connect it to a light errand of some kind—picking up a quart of milk or meeting someone for joe. Plan some extra time, if you can. It's great to walk, but walking slowly is delicious. Choose a beautiful day. Dress in layers, so you can adjust your body temperature with your step. Wear comfortable footwear. And walk.

Because walking is a cure. When we walk we take our place in nature. We untie our minds and improve thought. We restore our humanity. So, walk. After all, it's what we were designed to do.

Originally published in Salon, April 8, 2009.

27

WHAT'S REALLY IN YOUR SHAMPOO

THERE ARE TWO TYPES of ingredients in shampoo. One type cleans your hair. The other type strokes your emotions. I'm holding a bottle of Pantene Pro V, one of the world's most popular shampoos. Of the 22 ingredients in this bottle of shampoo, three clean hair. The rest are in the bottle not for the hair, but for the psychology of the person using the shampoo. At least two-thirds of this bottle, by volume, was put there just to make me feel good.

The world spends around $230 billion on beauty products every year. Of this figure, $40 billion go to shampoo purchases. North Americans blow almost $11 billion on shampoo and conditioner each year. So most soap manufacturers aren't willing to rely on a product that merely works. The bigger job is convincing the consumer that their soap is adding value to the consumer's life. So shampoo bottles include extra concoctions aimed at convincing the man or woman in the shower that the soap is more "luxurious" or "effective." Because beautiful hair doesn't just happen.

Have you got the greasies? One shampoo ingredient is all you need: detergent. Detergents are chemicals designed to bond to both water and grease. When the shampooer massages shampoo into the scalp, the detergent adheres to the grease. The detergent attaches to the rinse water and leaves, taking the grease (sebum) with it.

The most common shampoo detergents are ammonium lauryl sulphate and one of its molecular sidekicks, ammonium laureth sulphate. These viscous, yellow liquids, with the water of a shower, are enough to make your hair clean. They help stop the greasies.

Shampoo tends to use five factors to help the user feel good about it: shine, thickeners, lather, color, smell, coatings and exotic ingredients. Those ingredients, though they have nothing to do with cleansing, are part of the sell to convince you that something beautiful happens to your hair.

Consumers value shininess in nearly everything, including hair. For hair to shine, the cuticles of the hair must lie flat. Imagine a strand of hair as a stack of flimsy paper cups. When all the lips of the cup, called imbrications, lie flat, hair shines. Dull hair has the cups' lips sticking up. To get imbrications to lie flat, hair needs to be exposed to mildly acidic substances, so substances like citric acid are added to make the imbrications lie down and give hair that shiny look and to let yourself glow.

Consumers believe that thick is better. Which may explain why George Bush was a two-termer. Shampooers trust the velvet heft of the shampoo in the palms of their hands. So five of the 20 ingredients on the list are there because they help thicken the soap. Thickness also guarantees that people use more shampoo than necessary. There's salt, glycol distearate, cetyl alcohol, ammonium xylene sulfonate and others: body on tap.

And where would we be without suds? Cleaning agents do tend to foam a little when they're used, but the bubbles don't affect the cleansing much. However, the extra lather helps convince the shampooer that the soap is working. Lathering agents are added to boost the suds, chemicals like cocamide MEA. This little devil, besides being toxic in a few ways, also helps the lather to stay once it's been raised, a sudsy Viagra, with the help of known associates like the plastic PEG-7M. Great lather for great-looking hair.

Consumers tend to believe that good things must also be pretty. So shampoo manufacturers add colors, like purple and green, with reflective particulates to form blossoming clouds. Colors are often a problem either for humans or for the environment, like good old red dye no. 3, banned in 1990, eight years after a number of reliable studies revealed its cancer-causing tendency. Don't hate it for being beautiful.

Smell is important, because after the bathers have washed their hair, smell reminds them that the soap has done its job. Gee, some hair smells terrific. Smell is often associated with a brand, and smell helps to form the most intimate psychological connection a soap can make with its user. But the more "natural" the smell, the less natural the machinations behind it. That lovely apple smell has about as much to do with apples as Dick Cheney with world peace. And fragrance can be particularly dangerous because it's not specifically labeled. It's a combination of ingredients that could be harmless, on one hand or, on the other, noxious.

Once the natural oils have been removed from scalp and

hair, shampoo often replaces them with conditioners derived from animals or plants. These conditioners coat the hair and smooth its surface. The bottle of shampoo I'm holding uses dimethicone to coat the hair (it also helps to thicken the shampoo). It's a silicone-based chemical that coats hair and skin. You'll also find it in caulking, Silly Putty, and herbicides. No more tears. No more tangles.

Some shampoo sounds more like chicken marinade than shampoo, boasting of vitamins, minerals, protein and herbs. But, the vitamins and minerals and exotic extras play a useless role. So whether the shampoo brags that it is "infused" with real beer, exotic proteins, vitamins, antioxidants, or extracts from some fabulously endangered species, the additive saturates the users' minds, not their hair.

All these ingredients would go bad were it not for preservatives, a chemical equivalent of the right to bear arms. Sodium benzoate, for example, is handy because it kills nearly every living thing that might start to grow in a shampoo bottle. Ironically, in most cases the detergents won't go bad. It's the psychological ingredients that need preservation.

And these chemicals are tough to track down because tracking chemical names, it turns out, is a little like tracking criminals. Most have several aliases and fake IDs, play a role in many different products, and are shifty when caught and questioned. Some have long toxicity records; others are suspects in a range of problems. Of the 22 shampoo ingredients in my hand, all except three have proved to contribute, or are suspected of contributing, to health or environmental problems. Most of these ingredients, though known toxins, are permitted for use, because the small quantities limit human and environmental exposure.

Most of the ingredients in shampoo "may" cause health concerns. The word "may" is used because most chemicals have never been tested. Of the more than 80,000 chemicals registered and used in the U.S. since World War II, fewer than 500 have ever been properly studied for their effects on humans and the environment. So it's hard to say exactly how dangerous it is to use shampoo every day.

In May 2008, Jane Houlihan, director of research for the Environmental Working Group, reported on the dangers of cosmetics and personal care products to a House subcommittee. She believes that these products, including shampoo, are the biggest source of human exposure to dangerous chemicals. According to Houlihan, "companies are free to use almost any ingredient they choose in personal care products, with no proof of safety required." Consumers are not properly warned of possible dangers because of a "lack of standards and labeling loopholes." Let's just say that the less you hang out with any of these chemicals, the better off you are, we all are.

Mount Sinai Hospital reports that 2.5 billion pounds of toxic chemicals are released in the U.S. each year, the equivalent of 37,100 tanker trucks of noxious chemicals. A lot of these chemicals are released from homes every day. Daily, 45 billion gallons of wastewater go down the drain to be treated at one of the 16,000 water treatment plants in the U.S. But wastewater plants are designed to handle only the major pollutants. They can't remove the diversity of chemicals that humans flush every day.

This is the big problem with the shampoo ingredients: When a man rinses his hair, all the ingredients wash down the drain, carrying the grease to boot. And as one man's shampoo travels down the pipe, it meets up with a woman's, and so on, and so on, and so on. At least 350 million gallons of shampoo and its unregulated ingredients flow down U.S. drains every year. And many of these chemicals flow straight into our freshwater systems.

Shampoo, for example, contributes to high levels of estrogen and estrogen-like substances (endocrine disrupters) in freshwater downstream of sewage treatment plants that damage fish populations and cause male fish to grow ovaries, a sort of liquid feminism. My hometown of Calgary, Canada, studied the fish downstream of where we add our treated sewage to the river and discovered that female fish outnumber male fish 9 to 1. Estrogen runs through it. One study identifies more than 200 chemicals that are still present in wastewater after treatment. But the problem is likely much larger: environmental damage is difficult to estimate because we're dumping chemicals into the environment that have never been studied.

As we get to know some of these chemicals better, we discover that they should not be trusted. Health Canada is proposing concentration limits for two common shampoo ingredients, siloxanes D4 and D5, aka, Octamethylcyclotetrasiloxane and Decamethylcyclopentasiloxane, respectively. D4 and D5 did make hair easier to dry, silky soft, and easier to work with. Also handy when making plastics and paint. Sometimes you need a little D4 or D5. Sometimes you need a lot. But

Health Canada suspects that D4 and D5 are affecting fish and aquatic organisms. But, oh, how hair shines.

So I can live without the bottled psychology. My new shampoo, Sunlight Dish Detergent, has just four ingredients. It's runny and slightly acidic, smells vaguely lemony, doesn't foam excessively and looks anemic. It's not perfect, just better. I need to apply it only once when I shampoo. With each shampoo, I use a 10th of the volume that regular shampoo requires. The bottle will last at least a year, as my last one did. And though its ingredients aren't worth celebrity endorsement, my hair gets clean and I expose my body and the environment to less risk.

Originally published in Salon, August 13, 2009.

28

NAVIGATING THE COUNTRY

THERE'S A HOUSE YOU should see," Gary says to me.

"Where is it?" I ask.

"It's just north of the Mackenzies' place," he says in a tone that should settle my question.

I look at him with confusion, because I've just moved to the country with my family, and I don't know the Mackenzies.

"To the northeast," he adds, hoping for clarity.

His instructions mean nothing to me. But this is how the country is reckoned. It is a landscape blanketed by relationship. Directions are given in terms of people.

In the city, one is found in the building one occupies. In the country, the building is found by the person who occupies it. In the city, addresses are a mathematic, geometrical approximation. In the country, it's about who you know and how you fit into the web of residents. It's also about having lived there for a while.

We've recently come from Calgary. Our last house address was a location code that required no knowledge of the people who live there. Any newcomer could find it. All one needs to know is that the first two digits of the building number are going to correspond roughly with the nearest cross-street or avenue. It's a clever system, designed to put an almost exact picture of where things are from the address.

That doesn't work out here. The building number of our new 911 address is six digits long. It's called a 911 address because emergency vehicles find their way to homes using them. If I tell ours to anyone who lives out here, they look at me quizzically. Locals don't use them.

So when I'm asked for directions, I tell people, "We're in the Osbournes' house." If they know the right family, that works. If they don't, I use an older name, one that's more deeply tied to the landscape: "We're on the road across from Dave and Jody's." Anyone who lives in the area knows exactly what I mean. A few older residents, once I locate myself, will say something like, "Oh, you're on the old Parkins farm."

Names in the city are chosen for their gravity, and what you can expect to pay for the houses in that area. Calgary's Mount Royal, for example, is out of my price range. Discovery is midrange. Then there are the less expensive neighbourhoods with big ambitions: Tuxedo, Tuscany, Mahogany. These are names designers and writers choose for products, similar to names such as Grape-Nuts or Grand Caravan. The country eschews these types of naming practices.

Mr. Burby lives up the road from us, and his family has lived there for three generations. Does it matter whether he keeps his place up nicely? Does it matter if he made great contributions to the community? Does it matter if his name has a handsome ring to it? No, no, no. Hence, the bridge after the bend in the road near his place is known as Burby Bridge.

The community centre nearby, Burby Hall. Millarville, the town we live close to, is named after Malcolm T. Millar, the original postmaster and rancher. Bragg Creek is named after the Bragg brothers.

Since names don't work for those of us who are new, we resort to a childish-sounding system of landmarks. Landmarks are used in the city, too. I might have told someone that, for example, we were across from the community centre, or near a mall. Out here, there aren't enough landmark buildings to use as markers, so the directions sound silly.

My wife was attending a women's meeting recently. When the relational directions failed, she was told to "take the first driveway on the right after the big hill. Drive straight until you pass a pile of dirt. Stop when you pass a field with three white horses in it, and take the driveway in the middle."

So it was with Gary. "You know that truck that's for sale off the 549?"

"Yes, that black Ford?"

"You mean the two-tone GM?"

"Sure."

"Turn right at that road. Go up to the top of the hill, and up about a mile, and you'll see a house with a shake front on the left-hand side. Brian built that place. You should see the inside of it. It's beautiful."

Gary realizes most of this information is going over my head, so he stops. "It's right across from the Mackenzies' place," he says, slightly frustrated.

"I'll check it out," I say. And I amuse myself a little later that morning by following his directions, and actually finding the house. I pull over. A cow that's out of its enclosure stares at me as it chews morosely, like one of my children after I've told a joke at the supper table.

The house with the shake front is a beauty. I turn to the left. "So that's the Mackenzie place," I say to myself. A whole new part of the map opens up for me. A few giant, golden marshmallows of hay bask in the pasture in front.

So goes my country education, a name at a time. But is it ever nice to be part of the next conversation when a location I now know comes up. I nod solemnly, as if I've known it all my life. I'm in on the map.

Each year we live here, our family name will grow and bind itself to the land. Our history synonymous with the soil we occupy. We'll become a landmark. One that makes the map.

Originally published in the Globe and Mail, Facts & Arguments,
April 30, 2010.

29

ALL ALONE WITH JUST ONE COLOUR

IT'S A MOONLIT MIDNIGHT. The snow is as deep as anyone has seen for the last twenty-five years, and the entire landscape is blue. Blue snow. Blue moon shadows, cast by blue trees, before blue foothills fronting blue mountains. A blue dog sniffing the ground in front of me. The odd star is bold enough to shine through the moonlit sky. And as I study them, they're blue, too, as is the moon. I sit for moments until it finally hits me: it seems I am alone outside with just one colour.

What I am seeing is variations of a single colour. The hue is blue. But the landscape is rendered in the many tints and shades of blue. All possible blues. I wonder, as I inventory all I see, is this possible? Is it possible to sit alone with just one colour?

As I think about it, I have had a few other moments alone with a colour. I enjoyed, for example, snorkeling at a pool near our house. My mom would drop me off at a neglected swimming pool. Often, I was their only patron. I loved being under the water with my mask, the blue-green all around me.

Two days ago, I was alone with just one colour for many moments because of weather. Where I live, we sometimes get blizzards where the snow falls thick and deep. And the falling pixels of snow colour everything. It is possible to be alone with just white in those instances. In a couple of cases, it's alarming. It's a situation we call a "whiteout" here, which means the snow is falling and/or blowing to the degree that one cannot see any other objects. One is literally walled in by white. All that white can mean isolates and threatens me.

Yesterday, I was alone with white, the horizon shut away by the white of falling snow, the trees, caked white with huge barbs of hoar frost, branches bent low with the weight. Billions of shades of white.

My favourite colours to be with are the blues and indigos of the late night and early morning. These colours begin and live between civil and astronomical twilights. Civil twilight begins when the trailing edge of the sun falls below the visible horizon, while the light is strong enough to continue to work outdoors without artificial lights. Colour exists in civil twilight. But after civil twilight ends, nautical twilight begins until the sun is 12 degrees below the horizon. Nautical twilight continues until the horizon is no longer visible—an important moment for sailors. After nautical twilight comes astronomical twilight, where the sun drops to 18 degrees past the horizon and the world becomes dark enough that astronomers can begin their work without the interference of the sun. From a little after the middle of nautical twilight to the middle of astronomical twilight, one can watch the din of colour melt into a single hue.

All natural colour is born before each sunrise, and dies after each sunset. At sunrise, the war of colour begins. The sky begins with blue and its shades and as it lightens one of the first colours is red or orange, opposites of blue. Day begins like a sports event, where the home team is introduced, and then the away team. The kickoff to a war of colour, a war that competes for my gaze and focus all day long. A war that is, sometimes, a joy to retreat from.

My 1973, lemon-yellow Pinto hatchback helped me be alone with one colour. I remember driving back from my job, several miles into the country, and when the panorama glowed with a single hue, I could turn off the exterior lights, and twist the knob to shut off the dash lights. Alone I'd drive, soaking in the dark interior of the car, gazing out on a world of only one colour.

But this morning, the world is indigo. The trees, grape. A plum-coloured moose, saunters with me down the road, with its lanky gait. The snow reflects indigo everywhere, on the ground, the tips of trees, piled high on the side of the road, varnishing mountain angles and spires. I stop the car, shut it off and step out. Not a sound of another living soul. Not an artificial light anywhere, in any direction. A lighter indigo to the east hints at where the sun might appear. But for a few more minutes at least, I will stand and take my shade with the rest of landscape. Alone and wordless, I go indigo.

Originally published in Freefall Magazine, Fall 2011.

END

BILL BUNN

teaches English at Mt. Royal University in Calgary, Alberta, Canada. He lives in a rural neighbourhood with his wife, three teenagers, and assorted dogs, cats, and other animals. He is the author of two books: *Canoë Lune*, an illustrated children's book, and *Duck Boy*, a young adult fantasy adventure.

CPSIA information can be obtained at www.ICGtesting.com
Printed in the USA
LVOW100334190313

324837LV00007B/19/P